Guidance and Support in Caring for the Elderly

Canadian Medical Association
Guidance and Support in Caring for the Elderly

Ann Rhodes

Grosvenor House Press Inc.
Montréal - Toronto

The publisher wishes to express its gratitude to **Parke-Davis** for an education grant which has helped to make the publication of this book possible.

Canadian Cataloguing in Publication Data

Rhodes, Ann, 1932 –
Caring for the Elderly

Issued also in French under title:
Prendre soin de nos aînés

Includes bibliographical references
ISBN 0-919959-50-4

1. Aged - Care 2. Aging 3. Aged - Health and Hygiene
4. Aged - Services for - Canada 5. Caregivers - services for - Canada
I. Canadian Medical Association II. Title

HV1475.R46#1990 362.6'0971 C90-093313-5

Published by

Grosvenor House Press Inc.
1456 Sherbrooke Street West
3rd Floor
Montreal, Quebec H3G 1K4

Grosvenor House Press Inc.
99 Queen Street East
Suite 302
Toronto, Ontario M5C 1S1

Cover concept by William D. Marler
Printed and bound in Canada by Tri-Graphic Printing (Ottawa) Ltd.

Contents

Foreword

Each year the population of Canada grows older. By 2001, about 13 percent of Canadians will be over the age of 65 years, and by 2021 this proportion will have risen to over 18 percent. But all elderly people are not the same. Some will continue to lead healthy, active and productive lives into their 80s and 90s; some will require a minimal amount of assistance in their daily living activities, but will still be able to live in their own homes. Others will require more constant care either in the homes of relatives or friends; still others will require institutionalized care. The difficult problem for relatives and friends of old people is deciding when and what type of assistance is needed and how to provide it.

In this book, Ann Rhodes, who has had more than her share of responsibility of looking after older relatives, has not attempted to provide all the answers to questions caregivers may have, but she does help to clarify the questions and show where help can be found. She provides down-to-earth advice on how to ensure that elderly people are being given good care while still preserving as much as possible their independence, confidence and competence. She also offers good advice on how caregivers can gain respite from sometimes overwhelming problems in providing that care.

The Canadian Medical Association is pleased to endorse this practical and informative approach to caring for elderly people. Health care is not the sole responsibility of health professionals; good health and good care demand the participation of everyone.

Marcien Fournier, M.D.
President
The Canadian Medical Association
December 1989

Preface

Caring for an elderly person can have many rewards, but it can also be frustrating. Often caregivers are stretched to their physical and emotional limits — a woman may be caring for adolescent children and an elder as well as running a home *and* holding down a job. Many also have difficulty finding the professional help those they care for need, often because they don't understand what kind of assistance is required. In this book, we will give caregivers some understanding of the aging process, help them recognize their elders' real needs, and show them how to find their way into the system to get the right professional assistance.

Most elderly people wish to remain independent and stay in their own communities. Helping them do so makes sense in both humanitarian and economic terms. It can cost more than $300 a day for an elder to stay in an institution, but given professional care costing perhaps $50 a week, that elder might be able to go on living at home. Leading gerontologist Blossom Wigdor states in her recent book, *The Over-Forty Society*, co-authored with economist David Foot, that between 15 and 20 percent of elders now in institutions could manage well in the community provided they had minimal assistance — be it help preparing meals or some nursing and other skilled care.

In one short book, it will not be possible to cover all the bases. As our society ages, more and more services and facilities for elders are coming on stream. An entire book could be written on some aspects of caregiving. But my colleagues and I hope we shall at least be able to point caregivers in the right direction at appropriate stages.

The greatest misconception about elders is that they age uniformly and that they are a homogeneous group. This is emphatically not so. Some people in their 80s and 90s lead vigorous and independent lives, meeting new challenges and making new friends. Others in their 50s or 60s are severely hampered by chronic conditions for which they need regular or constant care.

The subject matter of this book is presented along a continuum of care. Thus, the opening chapters help caregivers recognize the need for care and provide brief descriptions of the most common conditions of aging. Then we look at ways in which elders can help themselves, perhaps with some encouragement from caregivers. Subsequently, we discuss minimal help, daytime care, altered living arrangements, and, finally, residential care.

Often those receiving care are referred to as elders. I and my colleagues like the term. It carries connotations of "elders and betters." As we will say again in this book, our elders constitute a truly grand generation. They have survived traumatic change in the world around them, and many of them have much wisdom to impart. They merit our care, our admiration, and our love.

Ann Rhodes

Acknowledgements

The list of those whom I want to thank is long. It includes all those who took the time to give interviews or otherwise help in the research; they are too numerous to list here but will know who they are. Among them are professional and lay caregivers who impressed me enormously with their caring, compassionate attitudes and elders themselves who shared their wisdom and their laughter. I would like to thank publisher Ian Burgham for giving me the opportunity to write this book and for the faith he thus placed in me, and editors Joan Irving and Christine Oddie, who joined the team late in the game but who did much to improve my copy and bring the project to fruition.

As well, I am indebted to the members of the advisory board whose critical review of the manuscript resulted in substantial improvements. I am especially grateful for input and counsel from the Canadian Pharmaceutical Association.

As a lay person, I feel highly privileged to have been given the chance to write this book, even more so to have it endorsed by the Canadian Medical Association, and I would like to record my great appreciation to Ms. Barbara Drew and Dr. Bruce Squires for their indefatigable input.

My special thanks to Fran MacDonald who, as always, did a first-rate editing job and was a pleasure to work with. Very special thanks to my research colleague, Jerri Yeomans, who did much to shape this book and to keep it on track, and finally to Pamela Marjorie Molyneux, my aunt, who has done a truly magnificent job of becoming an elder, and in so doing has taught me much about successful aging.

Ann Rhodes
December 1989

About the Advisory Board

The author and the publisher are indebted to the following Board members for their invaluable assistance in the creation of this book.

Dorothy C. H. Ley, M.D., F.R.C.P.(C), F.A.C.P.

Dr. Ley was an assistant professor of medicine at the University of Toronto. She founded the Palliative Care Foundation in 1981 and was its executive director until 1986. She was chairman of the Canadian Medical Association committee which prepared the report *Health Care of the Elderly: Today's Challenges, Tomorrow's Options*, and she now chairs the Implementation Committee. In 1988 she became the first woman to receive the Canadian Medical Association's medal of service.

Dr. Ley is a life member of the International Council of Women, and in 1989 she was elected Commander of the Order of St. Lazarus of Jerusalem.

Patricia Carruthers-Czyzewski, M.Sc. Pharmacology

Ms. Carruthers-Czyzewski participates on behalf of the Canadian Pharmaceutical Association in the Canadian Coalition of National Organizations, with interest in medication use and the elderly person. She set up and coordinated the Ottawa Valley Regional Drug Information Program from 1977 to 1980, and later established the clinical pharmacy services at the Ottawa General Hospital. She edited the French edition of the *Compendium of Pharmaceutical Specialties* for the Canadian Pharmaceutical Association, and now serves as the association's coordinator of professional development.

Catherine McCourt, M.D., F.R.C.P.(C), M.H.A.

Dr. McCourt received her undergraduate medical training, specialty training in community medicine and her Master's degree in health administration from the University of Ottawa. Currently, she is the associate director of the department of health services of the Canadian Medical Association (CMA). Dr. McCourt coordinated the implementation program for the CMA's 1987 report, *Health Care for the Elderly: Today's Challenges, Tomorrow's Options*. She served as military medical officer at the Canadian Forces Base in Ottawa from 1978 to 1981.

Norman Kristjan Blackie, M.D., B. Arch, D. Arch

Mr. Blackie is executive director of the Canadian Association on Gerontology and teaches at the University of Manitoba in Winnipeg. From 1980 to 1983 he was the associate director of the National Policy Centre on Housing and Living Arrangements for Older Americans at the University of Michigan. In addition, he has lectured at many other universities on gerontology and architecture. Mr. Blackie was President of the Manitoba Association on Gerontology, and he has served on numerous other boards and committees.

Guy Lacombe, M.D., F.R.C.P.(C.), C.S.P.Q.

Dr. Lacombe is currently Assistant Professor for the Internal Medicine and Geriatrics Department at the Centre Hospitalier Universitaire de Sherbrooke and Head of the Geriatric Assessment Department at Hopital d'Youville. Dr. Lacombe, who has been teaching geriatrics since 1985, is also a committee member for the Post-Graduate Geriatrics Training Program set up jointly by Université Laval and Université de Sherbrooke.

1

Assessing Change

The manner of giving is worth more than the gift.
Pierre Corneille

"This woman in her late 80s had been managing independently until she had two strokes. Because she had no close relatives, a cousin stepped in to help out while she was recovering in the hospital. She gave him power of attorney over her affairs. He believed she was no longer competent to take care of herself, so he gave up her rented apartment and spent some of her money.

"In fact, the woman made very good progress and was able to get about with a walker. She showed a good understanding of financial matters and so revoked the power of attorney and resumed control of her own affairs."

The speaker is Carolyn Glaze, a social worker with the Toronto Regional Geriatric Assessment Program team. At the request of family members or a physician, she goes to an elderly person's home to determine the basis of the problem that has been brought to her attention. Her appraisals, and her solutions, can be surprising.

She finds that family members and other untrained observers often misdiagnose difficulties of the elderly, frequently mistaking minor impediments for major problems. That, says Glaze, is because of our stereotypical view of old age. We expect the elderly to become physically frail and mentally impaired and to start withdrawing from the world. However, many retirees retain their physical and mental capacities until very late in life, and remain highly active and involved.

Dr. Michael Szul, a member of the same assessment team, notes that the very old are likely to be tough. "Many grew up without indoor toilets, without electricity, without the telephone," he says. They have also witnessed enormous changes in the world, from the development of radio to the threat of nuclear annihilation and environmental decay, and have survived those changes without being traumatized by them. They truly merit our respect.

Assessing the Problem

But you are concerned about a particular person who is not functioning as well as she or he once did. You need to know what's really wrong, but how do you find out? To start, observe, observe. Listen closely and search for clues. Even then you will almost certainly need help — perhaps from a professional assessor or the family physician.

You want to identify the change in the person that is worrying you. Has there been a physical change, such as pain or stumbling; is the change psychological, such as depression or confusion; or is it behavioral, such as forgetfulness or withdrawal?

Bear in mind that your perspective is highly personal. You are likely to compare your elder with another memorable aging person (a neighbor who was cantankerous; a great-uncle who took up painting). Biases — cultural as well as stereotypical — may cloud your judgment. An elder who has suddenly taken to sitting and reading may not seem "feisty" enough, if you have been reading magazine articles about 85-year-olds who are still playing golf.

Physical Changes

Some physical difficulties may not require any medical intervention whatsoever.

You may become alarmed because an older person starts falling. But look at the clues before attributing the cause to illness. The villain may be something as simple as a slippery floor, especially one with a throw rug on it. It may be a poorly lit staircase or an unstable chair the elder grasps for support. Painful calluses or ill-fitting shoes can also contribute to unsteadiness.

Reaching for an object on a high shelf may result in a fall. So may standing up too fast, which can cause a swift drop in blood pressure. Maybe there's just too much clutter in the home. The person is falling because, if eyesight is not as good as it once was, he or she does not see things lying around.

Falling, then, might be prevented by merely tidying up, adding more light, or suggesting new footwear. Many elderly women have to be persuaded to exchange their high heels for running shoes, but they are glad when they do switch.

When a fiercely independent old person suddenly starts complaining a great deal about aches and pains, you may be hearing a cry for attention — and not for attention to aches and pains. As Szul explains, "It is far more acceptable to say, 'My joints are hurting me,' than 'My grandchildren never come to see me.' I've never had elders complain of that spontaneously. But if I ask who comes and how often, they tell me. Then I ask, 'If you were the grandchildren, what would you do?' And they always burst into tears. Then they can express their innermost feelings."

The secret here is to have a good talk about events in an elderly person's life until you find the source of the distress. It may be worry that a child's marriage is on the rocks or unhappiness about the company a grandchild is keeping. It may be profound anxiety about money. It may be that this aging person is terrified of becoming dependent.

Psychological Changes

You are unlikely to be able, on your own, to assess the causes of psychological changes: they are too complex. But you can be aware of this complexity and seek appropriate professional guidance.

One of the most common troubles afflicting the elderly is depression. Yet, depression is by no means a single condition with a single remedy. Numerous physical illnesses can induce it. (These include cardiovascular disease, cancer, thyroid problems, hepatitis, and infections such as tuberculosis.) A diet deficient in protein and/or the B vitamins can also cause depression.

Medication may be the problem; depression is a side effect of many drugs prescribed to the elderly. Or, the problem may have psychological roots. Old people often feel lonely and isolated from society at large. Women, for instance, who were first and foremost homemakers may be depressed because no one needs their care any more.

Financial concerns can also contribute to depression. Money may be in short supply or have run out. Carolyn Glaze says she frequently sees well-to-do old people who save every elastic band and bit of string for fear they won't be able to make do. The point here is that there are as many causes for an emotional difficulty as there are treatments.

When an elderly person starts exhibiting memory loss or confusion, you may jump to the conclusion that she or he has Alzheimer disease or some other form of dementia. Be careful of snap judgments. "I've been asked to see a patient this weekend," recounts Dr.

Colin Powell, a specialist in geriatric medicine in Winnipeg. "This man is said to be demented, but a month ago he was walking around looking after himself and doing fine. Whatever else he has, he certainly doesn't have dementia. Dementia doesn't grab you in a month. It progresses slowly."

Even professionals are not infallible when it comes to recognizing Alzheimer disease. Dr. Roy Fox, a specialist in geriatric medicine at Dalhousie University in Halifax, tells of one woman diagnosed as having it. "Essentially, she became a recluse, doing nothing for herself, and becoming totally dependent on her family. Five years after the diagnosis, her memory was the same as it had been before. She was mildly forgetful, but labelling her as a victim of Alzheimer disease had had an extremely adverse effect on her behavior and that of her caregivers."

Memory loss can have a number of causes: it may be caused by hypothyroidism, or by atherosclerosis in blood vessels leading to and within the brain. An elderly person who takes several drugs or who is not getting enough vitamin B^{12} or folic acid may experience memory problems. The list could go on and on.

In addition, some loss of memory is normal to the aging process. And memory loss is often selective; an elderly person may well remember the happy events of 40 years ago but forget doctors' appointments during which he or she anticipates some discomfort.

Behavioral Changes

Withdrawal from friends and activities may be associated with aging, but it is not a symptom of aging. Maybe the person no longer wants to visit or dine out because poorly fitting dentures make it difficult to talk clearly or eat. Maybe the elder is embarrassed by hand tremors caused by Parkinson's disease. Or, maybe failing eyesight leads to fear of tripping over objects, being unable to recognize people, or eating messily.

An elderly person who has fallen hard once is likely to be worried about doing so again. "Just one severe fall can cause fear of falling," says Glaze. "That person may be afraid to even step out the door."

Generally speaking, withdrawal is more often found among the very old than among the recently retired who tend to have the hobbies, activities, money, and health that enable them to remain active. But a formerly active elderly person may suddenly become withdrawn and passive, especially after an illness. In such a case, try to find out if the family physician or other specialists involved in treatment advised a change in activity levels. Fox cites a patient who had such severe peripheral vascular disease that he had lost both legs and had to use artificial limbs. He also had heart disease, for which he was admitted to hospital. Complications set in; four weeks later he was still in hospital, in extremely weak condition, and taking many drugs. One of the doctors treating him said, "If you try to get back on your artificial legs, you'll kill yourself." The man later became Fox's patient and chose to believe Fox's reassurances that he *could* walk again. As Fox explains, "For him, life just wasn't worth anything unless he could move around and be independent. In fact, he is moving around and he's doing very well."

A normally even-tempered person who suddenly lashes out at a caregiver or family member may be expressing anger at the aging process. If you are on the receiving end of such anger, try not to let it upset you. Instead, help the elder express that rage; unvented anger can lead to depression. Szul advises: "Sit down and ask the person what life used to be like and what it's like now. Ask in what ways they feel good and what their disappointments are." Talking helps pinpoint the problem as well as relieve the stress.

If the elder shows signs of mental impairment, however, you will need to seek professional assistance.

Getting Elders to Accept Help

As you study your elders and their friends, you may have to abandon another stereotypical view: that elderly people tend to become hypochondriacal and to whine a lot. Some do become whiners, but assessors say they far more commonly see stubbornly independent people who will conceal problems in order to retain their independence. Whiners probably always whined a bit, and the independent were probably always independent. And there goes another myth. Age does not change elders and so homogenize them.

The stubbornly independent can give problems, of course. This writer has in mind a grand elder in her mid-80s, bent almost double by a disease of the spine, and in severe pain from ulcers on her ankles. When she thought no one was watching, she showed signs of pain. When anyone else was present — and especially when that other was her family physician — she hauled herself almost upright, almost managed to conceal her limp, and, with a broad smile and eyes shining, said, "I am just *fine!*"

One solution here is to call in the person in the white coat. Many elders have great respect for doctors, and where you may not be able to persuade an elder to have a night light and a commode (portable toilet) in the bedroom, and a grab bar on the wall so she or he can swing directly from bed to commode, the elder may readily obey the doctor. (Incidentally, this arrangement solves two common problems: nocturnal incontinence and dizziness and falls resulting from standing up too fast.) Sometimes, too, an elder may more readily accept ideas from a grandchild or from friends than from a daughter or son.

Or you might remark casually that Mrs. Johnson down the street had just this problem but came up with the neat idea of a grab bar and a commode. "This is likely to work if your elder knows Mrs. Johnson," Michael Szul says.

The Caregiver's Response

Working out solutions to the kinds of problems we have been discussing can take more time and patience than you may have. If you are starting to anticipate a greater increase in your responsibilities than you think you can handle, take heart. There is plenty of help available to you and to the elder you care for, as you'll learn. But you must confront a very important question: Should *you* give the care? If you are the prime caregiver to an elderly person, ask yourself if this is wise and if you're filling the role well.

For instance, if your elderly charge has become passive and dependent, could you be the reason? Perhaps, with your children grown and gone, or never having had children, your need to nurture is not being met and you're being too protective. Perhaps you are invading your elder's privacy and generally interfering. Privacy equates with independence. Your well-meaning compulsion to nurture may be proving stronger than your common sense.

Roy Fox emphasizes that caregivers and others commonly perceive an old person's condition to be worse than it is. "So caregivers become over-protective. They'll say, 'Well, I can't leave him alone because he might do such and such.' And yet he would probably be quite all right left alone."

But if you, the caregiver, are becoming progressively more exhausted, and the person you're looking after is rapidly becoming more debilitated, take a deep look at the situation and then discuss it with someone who specializes in geriatrics. (Geriatricians specialize in treating the medical problems peculiar to old age, while gerontologists study the problems of aging in all their aspects.)

You may be wearing yourself out providing help because of some kind of guilt. The aging person who gave up so much for you can no longer enjoy what you have: good health, a happy marriage, many friends. "Most caregivers do have love and affection for the elderly," says Michael Szul. "They feel they are not doing enough, yet if they *do* enough, they resent the demands made on them. And they can't admit to that resentment."

Changing Relationships

Being an appropriate caregiver may mean making changes in a longstanding relationship. This is always difficult, sometimes impossible. For all the love that passes between the caregiver and the elder, there may still be conflicts.

If your relationship with an elder is deteriorating, you may find the worksheets (in appendix A) to be helpful. They are intended to stimulate open discussion between elder and caregiver. The elder will set down a thoughtful assessment of her or his feelings, physical condition, and needs. You will assess your ability and suitability to meet those needs. You should both take plenty of time to think over your answers, then exchange worksheets and talk about the results privately or with a professional counsellor.

Professional involvement may be useful if an elderly person does not recognize the need for change or is resisting it. Not all elders acknowledge that age has made them infirm and less capable of handling their own affairs. Many simply do not want to change roles. Thus the caregiver must search for a way, not to make elders accept the change, but to make them active participants in it.

The two of you may have to air some old resentments — shake the skeletons in the closet — in order to work out the differences in perception. But in the process, you may find the start of a new, caring relationship.

Sharing the Load

Make no mistake, it is distressing to watch older people slowly deteriorate. But if it distresses you, how much more is it distressing them? Your own feelings should take second place, especially if part of your reaction is based on fear of your own aging.

If you're having trouble with your role, one solution may be to create a caregiver team to lighten your load. This can be a family affair. Some families do this well. Others find it difficult and need the help of a professional to pull together a team.

The team can also include friends or neighbors. In some neighborhoods and apartment complexes, networks of seniors plug the gaps that the caregivers have trouble filling. The young need to learn about aging, too. If you can assemble a caregiver team that includes children, everyone involved will benefit from the learning experience.

Finally, there are caregiver support groups in some communities that provide opportunities for caregivers to discuss their experiences and share not only the problems but also the solutions.

Where to Turn

The family physician can help in making a diagnosis or in referring the older patient to an appropriate assessor. There are geriatric assessment teams in every province, and their numbers are increasing rapidly. The caregiver can approach some teams directly, others request that a family physician make a referral. Assessments are usually covered by government health care plans.

The National Advisory Council on Aging (NACA) distributes, free of charge, a publication entitled *Geriatric Assessment: The Canadian Experience.* A list in the appendix gives the names and addresses of more than 100 hospitals and centres out of which teams operate, and this list is by no means complete. Write to the NACA at Room 340, Brooke Claxton Building, Ottawa, Ontario K1A 0K9. Alternatively, call the department of social work at your local hospital; staff there can probably tell you if there's an assessment program in your area. Members of the Victorian Order of Nurses (VON) do assessments, as do most occupational therapists and public health nurses.

Occupational therapists (OTs) will do home assessments. While not qualified to assess anyone's state of health, the OT can judge whether an elderly person is able to function adequately in his or her home and recommend changes where needed.

The assessment services of an OT are usually covered by government insurance when a doctor makes a referral to a hospital or other health care institution. There is a fee when you hire an independent OT directly. Listings for OTs appear in some Yellow Pages. Or you can write to the Canadian Association of Occupational Therapists at 110 Eglinton Avenue West, 3rd Floor, Toronto, Ontario M4R 1A3.

To find out if there is a caregivers' support group in your area, contact a local branch of the VON, public health nurses, or members of assessment teams. Or request information from the department of social work at a nearby hospital. For a list of publications and video titles that provide information on assessing the elderly and on the role of the caregiver, turn to appendix B.

2

Common Conditions of Aging

The first of earthly blessings, independence.
Edward Gibbon

"It's wonderful what they can do today," Margaret Byers says happily. She lives in an apartment on the Northwoodcare complex in Halifax, and is talking about a lens implant she had some seven years ago to restore vision in one eye. Now, at age 77, she is calmly preparing to have a similar operation on the other eye.

Byers is just one of many older people who are doing it right. They simply don't accept that they must live with debilitating ailments. They know that, whether the problem be failing eyesight or hearing, insomnia or sore feet, it can very likely be treated.

Let's take a look, then, at some of the ailments that commonly start to bother people in later life, and see what can be done to prevent and correct them.

Eyesight

As people age, the specialized cells of the eye are no longer able to perform as they once did. Many elders need bifocals for close vision. Others may develop cataracts or glaucoma.

Cataracts cause the lens of the eye to become opaque. Light can't get through the lens so sight becomes hazy. A cataract can often be seen — it's a kind of milky film in the eye.

Treatment for advanced cataracts involves removing the entire lens so that light can once again pass through. Some patients will have a lens implant (as Margaret Byers did) or wear glasses after the procedure. These days cataract removals are routine and are performed on an outpatient basis in the doctor's office.

Anyone who has glaucoma may notice no symptoms at all during its early stages. Later, he or she may complain that lights seem to have a halo around them or that vision has become impaired or distorted.

What is happening here is that fluid pressure is building up in the eye. If it is allowed to continue, blindness is inevitable. But if glaucoma is found early, it can usually be controlled with eyedrops or medication.

Elders should see an ophthalmologist once a year; this specialist will do a simple and painless check for glaucoma as well as the usual vision tests. Of course, if an elder's vision deteriorates suddenly, a specialist should be consulted immediately. This is especially important if an elder notices a change in vision after starting a new medication.

Hearing

Gradual loss of hearing is almost to be expected with advancing age, though it is more common among men than women. The decline is most commonly due to the loss of nerve fibre and is often referred to as nerve deafness. First to be lost is the ability to hear high-frequency sounds such as high musical notes. The ability to hear consonants in general conversation goes next, though the person will often hear the vowels. Elders may not recognize they have a hearing problem until someone else points it out to them.

Even a slight loss of hearing should be checked by a physician without delay. There may be an inflammation requiring treatment or a more serious neurological condition. Some drugs can also cause hearing impairment. Often though, the cause is a wax buildup in one or both ears, which a physician can usually syringe out.

Many people cope successfully with loss of hearing by wearing hearing aids. If an elder is not aware how light-weight and small today's models are, they should be encouraged to explore this market. Most are better off wearing an aid than struggling to learn lip reading (if they can). If an aid is prescribed and the wearer tosses it away in disgust, saying it doesn't work, explain that the hearing mechanisms in the ear may take a while to adjust to new sound levels and that persistence is necessary.

Oral Health

A Quebec study showed that 80 percent of those over 65 had not been to a dentist for five years; an Ontario study showed that, of elders living in the community and still having natural teeth, one in three needed fillings and one in five needed extractions.

Why are the elderly so reluctant to see a dentist? Perhaps because they do not know that dental treatment today is almost entirely painless. Some may fear the cost of treatment. (To date, only the Alberta and the Yukon health care plans provide help with payments of dental care for those over 65. However, some dentists will discount elders' bills, usually by about 10 percent, and some also accept payments in instalments.)

Dental problems and gum disease can cause severe malnourishment. Other diseases such as cancer of the tongue or lip may be incorrectly associated with toothache. Clearly, older people should have regular dental checkups or, if soreness develops and persists, see a dentist right away.

Dentures, like hearing aids, are often appropriate. Many elders already have them and may just need better help setting up a good hygiene routine. Others would benefit by obtaining dentures, or replacing old ones.

Here are a few tips on oral care for older people:

- A facecloth put in the basin when cleaning dentures will prevent breakage if they're dropped.

- If drugs cause a dry mouth, saliva substitutes are available. Avoid mouthwashes that contain alcohol; they will cause more dryness. Ask the pharmacist to recommend a fluoride rinse.

- If stiff hands make it hard to grasp a toothbrush, get a small rubber ball, make a hole in it, and put it on the end of the handle.

Foot Care

Older people often have trouble caring for their feet because they cannot reach them. Caregivers can usually do nail cutting and other simple procedures. With one exception: elders who have diabetes or poor circulation in the feet and legs should have all foot care — even nail cutting — done by a podiatrist, or chiropodist.

Corns and calluses, probably the most common problems, are most often caused by ill-fitting shoes. A gentle rub with a pumice stone after soaking the feet for 10 minutes in warm water may remove calluses in their early stages. If not, see the family physician.

And always consult her or him before trying any home remedies.

Bunions occur when the big toe joint swells and the bone enlarges and protrudes. (Men seldom get bunions because they usually wear sensible shoes.) The usual prescriptions are surgical shoes and, perhaps, medication. Much rarer is bunionectomy, a surgical procedure that shaves off some of the excess bone.

Here are some practices that will help keep feet healthier:

- When sitting, exercise feet by rotating them at the ankles and by alternately stretching and contracting the toes.

- Dry feet carefully after washing, especially between the toes where fungal conditions and infections often start. Then be liberal with a fine talcum powder (baby powder is excellent).

- Use a foot bath; one with vibrating pads to place the feet on yields an especially pleasant sensation. Follow with a massage of the feet using a lotion specifically formulated for the purpose.

- Trim nails flat across the top to prevent ingrown toenails.

Varicose Veins

Swollen and twisted veins occur most often in the legs. Blood pools in the veins, widening and lengthening them and causing the typical knobbly appearance. They can be quite painful.

Elastic bandages which support the veins and improve blood circulation can relieve the pain. Or medication may be taken to help circulation by shrinking the affected veins. More rarely, the person may undergo surgery to remove the veins.

Varicose veins are also quite commonly found in the rectum, in the form of hemorrhoids. Today, they can be removed during a simple procedure done under local anesthetic in the physician's office. Though the patient feels some discomfort, it doesn't last long. Many people, it should be stated, would rather control their hemorrhoids using topical medications that give temporary relief than discuss their condition with a physician. Surely comfort — physical and mental — should dictate which procedure is preferable.

Constipation

Bowel function is less vigorous with age, so some change in what might have been a lifelong pattern is entirely normal. Elders should not worry about this or resort to laxatives. They should try changing their diet to include more roughage — the natural laxative — and increase fluid intake and exercise. A person who has a bowel movement every couple of days, and feels comfortable, does not have constipation.

However, if the stools become too hard and difficult to pass, if they are black or bloody, or if there is rectal bleeding, medical help should be sought right away.

Constipation can result from overusing laxatives. The solution is to cut back gradually on the medication and, at the same time, gradually increase roughage, fluids, and exercise. Another cause of constipation is a fissure or tear in the wall of the anus. This can be repaired using a simple surgical procedure that requires only a short stay in hospital.

Obesity and Malnourishment

People require less food when they get older. Most make this adjustment quite naturally, but for some eating becomes a problem. They may eat too much and become obese, or they may not eat healthful foods and become malnourished. Either can have serious consequences.

Excess weight can place strain on the heart, spine, joints, and feet. Not eating well will aggravate the normal rates of loss of body fat and muscle tissue.

The section on diet in chapter 4 offers some information on the special needs of the elderly.

Insomnia

Older people may or may not experience change in their sleep patterns. Many elders simply require less sleep and may have to get used to getting up earlier or going to bed later. Less sleep is not the same as insomnia, which is not being able to sleep when it is needed and desired, and spending hours lying awake in bed.

People who take medication every evening to make them sleep should look carefully at their diet. Caffeine and alcohol are two major contributors to insomnia that should be cut out. Caffeine prevents sleep from starting, and alcohol may aggravate early waking. And both caffeine and alcohol may interact with prescription drugs.

There are ways to promote a good night's sleep, no matter how many hours of it an older person needs. Daily physical exercise, preferably in the open air, is one; it should be taken earlier in the day, since it may produce wakefulness if taken late in the evening. A warm, relaxing bath at bedtime often induces drowsiness. So does a warm, milky drink. It's also important to make the environment conducive to sleep: secure rattling windows, turn off dripping faucets, and so on.

Incontinence

An estimated one million Canadians suffer from urinary incontinence. Suffer is the right word: most are so ashamed that they tell no one. Eleven out of 12 will not even seek help. They withdraw from the world because they fear losing bladder control in public. Many go into homes for the elderly for this reason alone.

Caregivers and elders alike should be told that some loss of urinary control with aging is normal. And that there are many ways to either reverse or alleviate the condition. Urge any older people who have noticed the problem to see a physician about it. Also point out that trying to alleviate the condition by reducing fluid intake can cause dehydration, which can lead to serious complications.

Incontinence can be slight, partial or total. In men, its major cause is enlargement of the prostate gland and it is very common. In women, weakened muscles are often the cause. The bladder also loses its ability to empty completely, which can lead to bladder infections. Other causes may be diuretics (water pills) or too large a consumption of liquids that act as diuretics — tea, coffee, cola, and alcohol. Excess weight, constipation, and some medications can also contribute to incontinence.

Treatment may involve simple surgery or the use of medications. And women especially can strengthen the affected muscles using Kegel exercises. They consist of alternately tightening and relaxing the muscles that support the bladder several times a day. Sufferers who become incontinent when stressed may also find it helpful to learn relaxation techniques.

For those who must live with some degree of incontinence, see the section on specialized aids in chapter 7.

Mental Senescence

This is more commonly known as memory loss. It happens to everyone in varying degrees and it has nothing to do with senility. It should not be a cause for major concern, but it often is. Many elders can cause quite a fuss over checking repeatedly to see if the stove is off, for instance. Since they cannot remember, they will have to check. It may be more annoying to you than to them.

The best way to handle memory loss is to accept it in an elder and to help him or her learn compensatory strategies. Lists are one obvious aid, but there are many others. In the case of the stove, a special light might be installed in the living area to warn if the stove *is* on.

The solution, once any of the above problems has been acknowledged, is often quite simple and painless. The trick is in creating an environment where such acknowledgements come naturally.

Where to Turn

Elders should continue consulting their family physician. If they wish to find specialists in geriatric medicine, dental care, or other fields, the physician will be able to make recommendations. Or they can consult a member of a geriatric assessment team who will be able to recommend other specialists.

Those who want more information on incontinence can contact the Canadian Simon Foundation, founded in 1986. Write P.O. Box 3221, Tecumseh, Ontario, N8N 2M4, or phone 1-800-265-9575.

3

The Aging Body and Health Crises

We are too many, too diverse, too complicated, and too new to assume that any description will cover any but a few of us. . . .We are different from each other in the same way we were different all our lives.

Yhetta Gold, gerontology consultant and a past president of the National Advisory Council on Aging.

You probably know active 70-, 80-, 90-year-olds who have sustained their interests, nurtured their social contacts, and maintained a good measure of independence. You may also have seen what happens when normal aging is interrupted by a health crisis, and these elders are beset by a flood of terrors and pain, not the least of which is helplessness and dependence. Some conditions cannot be reversed, of course, and here appropriate care includes acknowledging the impending death. Many situations, however, can be prevented, ameliorated, or reversed, and these conditions lose many of their terrors once they are understood.

As we have seen, normal aging includes a slow but measurable loss of function in all specialized cells and tissues, a process which occurs in absolutely everyone over the age of 40. Healthy living habits and appropriate care when needed can, however, postpone, slow down and/or compensate for these changes, affording a high quality of life until the proverbial ripe old age. Chapters 2 and 4 of this book emphasize these aspects.

Often enough, however, an older person experiences health problems more severe than those due to normal aging. These problems demand care from others as well as informed self-care. Although some conditions may be temporary, such as the effects of a fall or a bout of flu, others may be permanent, such as deafness or diabetes. And some conditions, such as Alzheimer disease or liver cancer, mark the transition to palliative care and the beginning of the end of life.

Many of the chronic disorders that are common among the elderly, such as hardening of the arteries and arthritis, are not due to old age alone and also occur in younger people. These conditions may be thought of as being due to years of prolonged wear and tear on organs and systems in the body, though why some people are afflicted by them and others are not remains a mystery.

Some health crises — notably accidents and certain transmitted diseases — can largely be *prevented.* In many instances of disease the condition itself can be *treated,* healed or improved, and where this is not possible, the most distressing or threatening symptoms can usually be *relieved.* It is here, within this sphere of preventable, treatable, and relievable conditions and symptoms, that informed and sympathetic cooperation between elder and caregiver can do much to maintain the pleasure of life and keep potential health crises at bay.

The elderly should not, therefore, give in to the view that physical ailments and deteriorating health must just be accepted and lived with. By promptly consulting a doctor if a physical disorder appears, most health problems and their accompanying anxieties can be brought under control with appropriate measures. Cataract operations, for example, often do wonders for people who are afraid that they are going blind, and anti-inflammatory medicines can bring great relief to arthritis sufferers.

The following paragraphs pinpoint, under individual body systems, a selection of common physical and emotional disorders that affect the elderly, together with symptoms and a brief description of treatment. Some of the illnesses have unknown causes, but the majority are due to the accumulated effects of poor diet, to the lack of physical or mental stimulation, to muscle, joint and blood vessel wear and tear, and to cigarette and alcohol abuse.

Digestive System

Constipation, poor nutrition (underweight), and obesity (overweight) are common but non-threatening complaints among the elderly and have already been discussed.

• Stomach and intestinal *ulcers* are more serious. Untreated, they are not only painful but can lead to dangerous internal bleeding. There are several widely prescribed medications that bring most ulcers under control, and surgery is usually possible if drug treatments fail. Since ulcers are notorious for coming back in patients susceptible to them, by far the best strategy in this instance is prevention: avoid recurrences through a combination of non-provocative diet and preventive medications.

Ulcers are usually benign lesions in that their disease process does not neither rampage out of control as cancer does.

• *Cancer* is a disease process in which cells lose their specialized functions and multiply rapidly, threatening the whole body. Cancer can develop in any part of the digestive system, but large bowel cancer is especially common and esophageal cancer is particularly life-threatening.

Timely surgical removal of cancer tumors can ward off or halt the disease, but this in turn depends on recognizing the cancer before it is far advanced. Pain, difficulty in swallowing, or digesting or defecating, bleeding, and unexplained loss of weight are all symptoms requiring a visit to the doctor.

Endocrine System

The glands of the endocrine system help regulate body functions by secreting hormones that speed up or slow down key activities at the cellular level. Although endocrine disorders have their most devastating effects in young people, there is one endocrine disease which is a serious threat to many older people — diabetes.

• *Diabetes mellitus,* as it is known to doctors, is a metabolic imbalance caused by inadequate levels or reduced effectiveness of the hormone insulin. Insulin is produced by the pancreas; it stimulates cells to absorb molecules of glucose, a simple sugar, from the bloodstream and to use it for energy. Thus, insulin is essential both for regulating glucose and for maintaining the correct level of glucose in the blood.

Diabetes has many signs and symptoms. They include high blood sugar, excessive thirst followed by frequent urination, tiredness, irritability, skin infections, itching of the vulva in women and of the penis in men, ulcers on the feet, and numbness and pins-and-needles of the hands and feet. Worse, diabetes threatens the retina of the eye (and in severe cases causes permanent blindness) and significantly adds to the dangers of poor circulation and of poor liver and kidney function.

Diabetes mellitus in the elderly differs from that in the young. In the young, only a tiny quantity of insulin is produced, and insulin injections must make up what the body requires. In the elderly, insulin is produced in normal or even increased amounts, but it has markedly reduced effectiveness. The outcome, however, is similar — the level of glucose in the blood rises to dangerous levels. For older people, treatment with medication is not usually required. The diabetes is controlled through a modified diet, one in which all foods containing sugar are sharply reduced.

If possible, an appropriate diet should be established through the collaboration of elder, caregiver, and doctor or nutritionist. No one should be worried if it takes a little time for the new diet to become routine; the eating habits of a lifetime do not disappear overnight.

In the meantime, a physician should attend to all the potential dangers of diabetes while the elder and caregiver look for ways to prevent complicating conditions, especially cuts, bruises, and infections of the lower legs and feet. For most people these are minor problems that quickly resolve, but for an older diabetic person with circulatory difficulty they pose a significant risk to health, and healing is certain to be slow and difficult. Thus, prevention is the sensible approach.

Genito-Urinary System

• *Prolapse of the uterus* is a common disorder affecting elderly women in which the uterus drops down from its normal position to the bottom of the pelvis. This occurs when the muscles and ligaments that support the uterus, bladder, and rectum have been previously overstretched as a result of a breech delivery or other difficult birth. The bladder may slip into the vagina; the rectum may push forward; or the uterus may descend into the vagina.

Common symptoms include incontinence of urine, the feeling of obstruction in the vagina, and pain in the pelvis. Treatment involves either the fitting of a vaginal pessary or surgical repair. Both techniques are quite safe and easy when compared with the chronic discomfort of the condition, and the relief is well worth any potential embarrassment.

• An *enlarged prostate gland* is the special gremlin plaguing older men. It is so frequent in men over 60 that doctors consider it to be the norm. It is also normal for the enlarged prostate to obstruct the flow of urine from the bladder, causing pain, frequent urination (especially at night), difficult urination, incomplete urination, and incontinence. The latter has been described in chapter 2.

Hormone therapy may be used to shrink an enlarged prostate or it may be reduced surgically. Complete surgical removal is carried out when it is extremely enlarged.

• *Cancer of the prostate* also requires surgery. This cancer need not be dangerous if diagnosed in time — another good reason to see a doctor if repeated urinary pain and difficulty appear.

• *Cancer of the cervix* of the uterus in women is more serious, but it too can be successfully removed by surgery if caught in time. Many elderly women are uncomfortable with the medical screenings available to detect the disease in its early stages. Nevertheless, they should be encouraged to undergo them regularly, as prompt diagnosis offers the best hope for successful treatment.

Joints

• *Arthritis,* the inflammation of a joint causing pain, swelling, and restriction of movement, is perhaps the leading cause of chronic disability in the elderly.

• *Rheumatoid arthritis,* likely to be a disorder of the immune system, is a progressive disease in which the lining of joints is inflamed, going on to destroy major joints throughout the body. Usually appearing between the ages of 20 and 40, its initial complaints include hot, red, stiff, swollen, and painful joints of the fingers and feet, above all occurring in the morning upon waking.

A doctor may prescribe anti-inflammatory drugs to halt temporarily further destruction and to relieve pain. Cortisone and similar drugs may be helpful in severe cases. Bed rest, the application of heat to affected joints (heating pads, warm water bottles), and physical therapy are also mainstays of current treatment. At an advanced stage, surgery that replaces severely deformed joints with artificial ones results in much improved mobility and greater comfort. As autoimmune diseases become better understood, there is a good chance that more effective therapies will become available.

• *Osteoarthritis* is a more common but less severe condition, appearing especially in women over 55, in overweight persons, and in those with a family history of the disease. The inflammation is limited to a few joints — usually weight-bearing ones — and the fingers, and does not spread throughout the body. Symptoms include pain, swelling, and deformity of the affected joint. In mild cases the pain disappears and, apart from some stiffness, there is only moderate discomfort. In severe cases mobility is affected, and there is a degeneration of muscle around the damaged joint.

Rest, anti-inflammatory and pain-relieving drugs, and care not to subject the diseased joint to undue exertion all help relieve symptoms. Weight loss is important to lessen the stress on hip, ankle, and knee joints. Surgery has become particularly successful in replacing an osteoarthritic hip or knee with an artificial one.

Bones

• The condition of brittle bones in the elderly is known as *osteoporosis.* This is a weakening of bones from a reduction in bone mass, whether due to the natural process of aging, to prolonged physical inactivity, to extensive use of steroid drugs, or to loss of estrogen secretion in the case of women past menopause. Calcium in particular is slowly dissolved out of bone tissue; this process may go undetected until a bone fractures.

Common symptoms include pain, persistent backache, easily broken bones, curvature of the back, and decrease in height due to the flattening of some of the vertebrae. The most important consideration in giving care is the prevention of falls and other accidents (see other chapters).

Treatment includes weight loss if appropriate, so that no extra strain is placed on the weakened bones. Overall physical fitness can be improved through judicious exercise. A modified diet rich in calcium is sometimes prescribed. If needed, painkillers help relieve pain. Estrogen replacement therapy is prescribed for some women, though this needs to be administered with care.

Blood Vessels

• Often called hardening of the arteries, *arteriosclerosis* is the most common disease of blood vessels in the elderly and the most frequent cause of death in persons over 65. A major cause is *atherosclerosis,* in which normally smooth artery walls start to roughen and collect deposits of fatty materials (including cholesterol) and possibly calcium. These materials both fill up and stiffen the arteries, impeding the flow of blood.

The main causes of atherosclerosis appear to be poor dietary habits (too many animal fats and other foods containing cholesterol, and too much refined sugar), smoking, lack of exercise, high stress levels, and irritation or damage to the artery walls. Atherosclerosis is also frequently associated with high blood pressure, diabetes, and a family history of the disease. Symptoms include shortness of breath, dizziness, chest pains, and signs of poor circulation such as leg cramps and cold hands and feet.

If caught in its early stages, atherosclerosis is often checked by improving diet, exercising more, and quitting smoking. If medication is needed, physicians prescribe drugs that lower the cholesterol level in the blood. They may also suggest ASA (aspirin) or another anticoagulant to help prevent obstructive blood clots from forming.

• *Thrombophlebitis* is an inflammation of a length of vein, usually in the leg, accompanied by an obstructing blood clot. It is a common complication of varicose veins; other causes include injuries to the vein and prolonged immobility. The most bothersome symptom is pain and sometimes a visible swelling if the vein is near the skin's surface.

Thrombophlebitis should be diagnosed and treated, as venous clots may otherwise be transported to more vulnerable sites in the body such as lungs, heart, and head. There are widely prescribed drugs to relieve the pain and anticoagulants to hinder the tendency of the blood to clot. The affected limb should not be constricted in any way, whether with bandages, tight socks, or garters, and no direct or sustained pressure should be applied to the affected vein.

• A *pulmonary embolism* is the migration of a venous blood clot through the heart into the arteries of the lungs where it forms an obstruction. It causes shortness of breath, sudden coughing, and sharp chest pain. If the embolus is small, symptoms usually appear on just one side; if it is large, severe pain is felt over the whole front of the chest, the lips may turn blue, the victim may spit up blood, and there may be shock or loss of consciousness.

In mild cases a confirming chest X-ray and treatment with anti-coagulant drugs are sufficient. In severe cases patients require hospitalization. Oxygen is administered to ease breathing and prevent further damage, and surgery is employed to remove the obstructing blood clot.

In the elderly especially, prevention is again the best medicine. A healthy life-style, care to avoid cuts and bruises, extra precautions while undergoing unrelated surgery, and perhaps an anticoagulant drug all help to avoid this potential health crisis.

High Blood Pressure

• High blood pressure or *hypertension* is the condition in which the arteries offer too much resistance to the flow of blood, just like water pipes which are too small, inflexible, or partially plugged with grime. If hypertension goes unchecked, the overworked heart as well as the weakened blood vessels become damaged. Hypertension also adds to the dangers of many other conditions, especially coronary artery disease.

The presumed causes of hypertension are numerous: heredity and overweight are certainly factors, as is arteriosclerosis. So is diet, where a high cholesterol or salt content is imbibed. High stress levels, caffeine, alcohol, diabetes, various drugs, smoking, and a variety of other disease conditions have all been suggested, even the candy, licorice!

Hypertension is usually discovered when a person undergoes a routine blood pressure check — a good reason for a regular physical exam. The physician confirms hypertension by a series of blood-pressure checks and then determines whether damage to the heart, lungs, eyes, or kidneys has occurred. Older people normally have a higher blood pressure than when they were young, but beyond a certain danger level it is necessary to treat it and to make changes in eating and living habits.

To bring high blood pressure down in mild cases of hypertension, the most effective non-drug therapy is to limit salt intake severely and to control weight. Ceasing to smoke and increasing one's exercise will also help. Where necessary, high blood pressure is treated with appropriate drugs. The doctor may prescribe a diuretic to stimulate the kidneys to eliminate excess salt and water and a drug called a beta-blocker to help relax the layer of involuntary muscle encasing the major arteries. Other medications are available that open up the interior of the arteries.

These medications are highly effective, but they must be taken long-term and they do have notable side effects, such as drowsiness, and interactions with other drugs. (A fuller discussion of drug side effects and drug interactions appears in chapter 5.)

It is vital that elders with hypertension take their blood pressure medication exactly as prescribed. Sometimes a patient whose blood pressure has come down decides to do without his or her medication. This is dangerous, since drugs do not cure hypertension but merely keep it under control. An elder who stops taking medication will probably find at the next checkup that his or her blood pressure has gone back up to its previous worrisome level.

Heart

Although arthritis is first, the condition next most responsible for slowing down the elderly is a failing heart. There are a number of distinct conditions:

- *Coronary artery disease* (CAD) is caused by a buildup of fatty deposits in the coronary arteries carrying oxygenated blood to the heart muscles. The arteries become narrowed and normal blood flow is restricted.

One manifestation of the disease is chest pain (angina). This usually strikes following stress or exertion, when the heart's increased need for oxygen cannot be met by the narrowed coronary arteries.

The pain is constricting, crushing, or numbing, starting across the upper chest and often spreading to the jaw and down the left arm. Discomfort may last only a few minutes.

If the angina is very mild, the only treatment necessary may be improving circulation by losing excess weight and stopping smoking. If the vessels have become quite narrow, the physician may prescribe an anticoagulant medication to reduce the likelihood of a complete blockage by a blood clot (heart attack) together with a powerful drug such as nitroglycerine to expand the arteries.

If the CAD is severe and unresponsive to drug treatment, the diseased artery can be replaced with a transplanted leg vein (coronary artery bypass surgery). Alternatively it can be opened up and stretched by inflating a tiny balloon in it temporarily (intraluminal balloon angioplasty).

• Some older people with CAD experience no symptoms until they have a *heart attack*. Attacks occur when fatty deposits or a blood clot completely blocks a coronary artery and cuts off the blood supply to part of the heart muscle. The major symptom is gripping or crushing pain that spreads from the centre of the chest to the jaw, neck, and arms. Although the pain, which comes on suddenly, resembles that of angina, it is not usually brought on by exertion and it does not subside after a few minutes' rest.

Treatment begins with immediate hospitalization; here an electrocardiogram and X-rays of the heart vessels are used to confirm the diagnosis and emergency resuscitation facilities are readily available. Treatment may be either medical or surgical or both. Powerful drugs to dissolve blood clots and prevent them from reforming are new weapons in the doctors' hands.

Heart tissue that dies from oxygen starvation during the attack is not replaced, so that the heart is permanently weakened. This occurs to some extent in more than half of all attacks. Further, the elder who has suffered one attack is at increased risk of having another. Thus many elderly people would be wise to adjust their living habits to the health status of their heart. To lower the risk of further attacks, and also to prevent angina, doctors recommend that weight be kept at the ideal for the individual's height. They also recommend that exercise be planned to improve the heart's efficiency, and that smoking be stopped.

• *Congestive heart failure* is the general term used when the heart simply cannot meet the demands placed upon it and fails to pump sufficiently, causing a characteristic pooling (congestion) of blood in the major veins. It is a common cause of death in both middle and old age and is brought on by an increased work load, other cardiovascular disease, or both.

In cases of a failing heart, both elders and caregivers should be concerned with the prevention of a crisis. This is done by avoiding sudden or excessive exertion, reducing salt intake, maintaining healthy living habits, and taking preventive medicines such as digitalis to stimulate heart muscle and vasodilators to open up narrowed veins.

Stroke

• A *stroke,* also known as a *cerebral infarct,* is caused by a disruption in the blood supply to a part of the brain caused by a blocked or burst blood vessel. It is uncommon before the age of 50 but becomes increasingly common thereafter.

A minor or partial stroke, in which the interruption of the blood supply is very localized or brief, results in only a minor loss of function. Although the symptoms usually clear up within a few days, minor attacks may occur again and again.

In a massive stroke there is a serious loss of function. Loss of consciousness, paralysis, and weakness of the right or left side of the body are its major symptoms. Treatment requires hospitalization. In time therapy may help restore movement to affected limbs, though in the elderly one arm or a leg often remains disabled. Even so, many patients eventually resume the basic activities of independent living.

Neurological Diseases

Adult brain cells neither reproduce themselves nor regrow when damaged; cell degeneration and cell death are therefore permanent. Since an imperceptible loss of brain cells is always taking place, it is normal to experience a gradual decline in memory, learning, and reasoning abilities; this has been referred to in chapter 2 under senescence. There are also a number of pathological processes in which brain cells die or lose function much more quickly, and some are mentioned here.

• *Parkinson's disease* is one of the better known. This is a relatively common neurological disorder, mostly affecting people over 50 and caused by the degeneration of the special cells in the brain that produce an important nerve transmitter called dopamine.

The symptoms appear gradually, the first being tremors in the hands, arms and legs, and a rhythmical nodding of the head. Later, the facial muscles stiffen, and the sufferer stares blankly with infrequent blinking. The limbs stiffen and the victim walks with a shuffling gait. There may be intellectual impairment, including memory failure, slowness of thought, and reduced problem-solving ability. Caregivers need to recognize that the affected elder will need progressively greater care as he or she becomes increasingly incapacitated, but that the time scale is one of years.

Though there is no cure, various anti-Parkinsonism medications compensate in part for the missing dopamine and offset the disability for a while. Drugs that relax involuntary muscles help reduce the tremors, and a substance called levodopa or L-dopa is converted inside the brain to dopamine, affording temporary relief to symptoms. Physiotherapy and an exercise program of walking or swimming help maintain muscle tone. New drugs and tissue implants in the brain may offer improved treatment in the future.

• *Alzheimer disease* is the most devastating and terrifying neurological disease of older age. Unlike other forms of dementia which progress more slowly, Alzheimer is a rapid deformation of brain cells that leads to disfunction and helplessness within a short time and death within a few years. There is no treatment, only control of some of the worst symptoms of dementia. Often the family cannot cope with an Alzheimer patient on its own, and the affected older person has to be put into an institution. Tragically, after a short time there is no "quality of life" to be conserved.

For everyone concerned, an early diagnosis that is as accurate as possible is important above all else. The earliest symptom of the disease is a drastic and sudden memory loss, noticeable week by week. If this is *not* diagnosed as Alzheimer, then vigorous examination, diagnosis, and treatment may be able to reverse the condition. If it is Alzheimer, the family and other caregiver(s) must begin the very difficult process of accepting the inevitable outcome. Alzheimer societies offer valuable support systems for families and caregivers who find themselves in this situation.

Psychiatric Illness

• *Depression* is the most common psychiatric illness of the elderly. Often it is provoked by retirement and the adjustment to a changed way of life or by the loss of a loved one. Some sufferers report a decrease in energy and a loss of enthusiasm for life; others experience as well an inability to sleep soundly, frequent crying, a loss of appetite, diminished interest in once-enjoyed activities, and a feeling of worthlessness.

In caring for depressed elders, don't try to manage alone, but seek medical help. Let your elders know you love them and need them. They should be encouraged to talk about anxieties and to express their feelings of despair. If you recognize that they are not improving or not coping with life, that they suffer from attacks of listlessness, or that suicide is a possibility, medical help should be sought immediately. The physician may prescribe small quantities of an antidepressant medication.

Caregivers must be extra attentive when elderly people are depressed, since they may feel that it is no longer worthwhile to maintain good habits of diet, sleep, exercise, recreation, taking the right drugs at the right times, and so on. During the two to eight weeks usually required to clear up a depression, caregivers must do extra checking to make sure that elders are not suffering in other areas of life.

Respiratory System

• The frail elderly are particularly susceptible to *pneumonia*, a viral or bacterial infection that causes acute inflammation of the lungs. Symptoms include high fever with rapid breathing, chest pain often on one side, dry cough, and production of sputum that may contain streaks of blood. Since the fever is the symptom that above all demands an immediate visit to the doctor, the elder and caregiver should remember that in many older people the normal body temperature is less than 37°C, so that a temperature of 38.5° may already be cause for alarm.

Once the diagnosis is confirmed by a physical examination and chest X-ray, the physician almost always prescribes an antibiotic if the pneumonia is bacterial, together with bed rest and the drinking of plenty of fluids. Since pneumonia is especially severe in older people and is a significant cause of death, hospitalization is common during the critical phases of this disease. Further chest X-rays and close follow-up will ascertain when there is a complete cure.

Elders who are known to be susceptible to respiratory infections in the winter should heed the rule that prevention is better than cure and guard extra carefully against chills and any other weakened condition.

• *Influenza*, a group of viral infections of the upper respiratory tract, is one of the leading causes of death among elderly people. Since influenza usually strikes during the winter months, in autumn elders should obtain vaccination against the latest strain of the disease. This will prevent or lessen the severity of the illness and also protect against secondary infections such as pneumonia. Note that some elders with other medical conditions cannot be vaccinated against influenza.

A sore throat, chills, loss of appetite, headache, muscle and joint pains, fever, watering of the eyes, dry cough, and nasal catarrh are the common symptoms. They are best remedied by rest, drinking extra fluids to offset dehydration from fever, and by taking fever reducers and perhaps analgesics for muscle pain. Antibiotics may also be prescribed to prevent complications such as pneumonia, sinusitis and middle ear infection.

• *Chronic bronchitis* is a long-term and slowly spreading inflammation of the bronchial tubes of the lungs that is marked by a persistent cough; its main cause is smoking but it can also stem from prolonged exposure to air pollution, particularly sulphur dioxide. Symptoms include coughing, malaise and fever, vague chest pains, phlegm production, wheezing, and breathlessness. It is somewhat more common in overweight people.

Quitting smoking, avoidance of inhaled irritants, and an increase in physical fitness reduce the severity of the symptoms and may halt the advance of the disease. Antibiotics prevent additional infection, steam inhalations and cough suppressants ease the coughing, and drugs which expand the air passages (bronchodilators) relieve and may even partially reverse the condition of breathlessness.

• *Emphysema* is a pathological accumulation of air in the lungs which causes chronic shortness of breath. This disease occurs more often among the very old and among people whose breathing difficulties are not compounded by overweight and heart trouble. It is caused by the thinning out and rupturing of the walls of the tiny air sacs in the lungs. At first there is labored breathing upon exertion. Later, as the destruction of the air sacs proceeds, breathing becomes difficult even at rest. Most of the damage is irreversible.

Smoking is the common cause. Treatment is similar to that for chronic bronchitis, with the addition of bottled oxygen to assist breathing in advanced cases. The physician should monitor the heart closely, as lowered levels of oxygen in the blood places an additional strain on the heart.

• *Lung cancer* has become so prevalent that it is now the leading cause of cancer death among older men. It has been conclusively linked to smoking and the inhalation of industrial pollutants. It has a poor prognosis, i.e. the standard treatments of surgery, chemotherapy, and radiation therapy have limited value in prolonging life and are often as debilitating as the disease.

Breast Cancer

• *Breast cancer* is the most common of all cancers in women: one in every 11 women in North America experiences it and it is the leading cause of cancer death among women. It appears to be linked to a number of factors, but particularly to the balance of different female hormones. Since there is no definitive cure and no prevention, regular examination to catch the disease in its early stages cannot be stressed strongly enough.

The cancer tumors in the breasts themselves are less life-threatening than those which have spread to other organs in the body (metastases). Preventing metastases depends in part on detecting cancerous lumps in the breast while they are still small. The best methods of early detection are regular self-examination and a relatively new technique called screening mammography. The latter uses X-rays or very powerful visible light beamed from the side to reveal masses of extra dense tissue in the breast. Such a mass in women over 50 years old is often not benign but cancerous.

Mastectomy (removal of the affected breast) and hormone manipulation are the standard forms of treatment, though modern practice is beginning to favor partial mastectomy (lumpectomy), plus auxillary dissections followed by radiation therapy. These therapies imply substantial changes in the lives of affected women, and many elders have had to learn how to live with their new circumstances.

4

Maintaining Health

The best insurance against disease is health.
Maurice Duplessis

Judy Radau is supervisor of the seniors' health team in the Scarborough, Ontario, health department. She tells a revealing story concerning a man who was dying of cancer and his wife who was legally blind. Several sons and a daughter — all married with their own families — lived nearby. "The family decided to take a palliative approach, wanting him to die at home," Radau says.

They achieved this in several ways. First of all, the daughter and the mother were very supportive of one another, and the sons provided good emotional backup. The family physician was also very supportive. As the end approached, Radau 's department sent in home care workers, and Radau went in herself twice a week to help the family deal with what was to come; the wife, already with sight loss and now facing the loss of her husband, was her prime concern.

After the man's death, Radau continued to visit his wife. "She did quite well. Certainly she mourned, but she started to rebuild her life. Later she went into a seniors' building and, with a little help, learned to cope on her own."

The family Radau talks about is typical. Most older people want to remain in their own homes as long as possible. The story also illustrates how this can be achieved, given strong family support and some professional help.

Unfortunately, however, Canada has a higher percentage of elders in institutions than any other western industrialized country — bad news, not only for them, but for all of us, since our taxes pay the high cost of institutional care.

There is good news too. More elderly people now remain in the community. And many more could do so if their caregivers realized just how much elders can do, with a little help, to remain physically and mentally healthy and thus stay in charge of their lives. This is the key to sustaining resilience as one ages.

The first step in ensuring a safe and effective approach to the many aspects of fitness is to enlist the support of a physician.

Working with the Physician

If older people in your care do not already see a physician for regular checkups, encourage them to do so. Sometimes "encouragement" might mean that you make the appointment and then accompany them to the doctor's office. Don't insist on going into the appointment with the elder, who has a basic right to privacy.

In his geriatric assessment clinic in Halifax, Dr. Roy Fox sees his patients alone first, unless they specifically ask that the caregiver be present. He then interviews the caregiver, "to get another perspective on the problem." Finally, he sees patients and caregivers together so no one feels left out.

It is especially important that you accompany an elder who has postponed seeing a physician in anticipation of bad news. If the news *is* bad, your comfort and understanding will help.

Keeping a Medical Diary

A medical diary can furnish a lot of useful information for the patient, the caregiver, and the physician. It does not have to be complicated; simply encourage the elderly person to jot down in a notebook how he or she feels each day and what kinds of food and exercise are taken. Any prescription or over-the-counter medications should also be noted when taken.

An older person may enjoy keeping this diary. Many are already great list makers (a habit often acquired in middle age). The list can help prevent over-medication: after looking in the notebook and seeing under the day's date, "Took two blue heart pills," the elder will not repeat the daily dose.

The diary may also show whether or not the elder is eating right and exercising regularly. If she or he is not, the physician may suggest a diet or make a referral to a dietician or nutritionist and prescribe a suitable exercise program.

Dietary Fitness

People's nutritional needs and ability to process food change as they grow older. Knowledge about the nutritional needs of the elderly is spreading fast, and many elders are now helping themselves and each other acquire this knowledge. For instance, in a nutrition program in Saskatoon called Seniors Helping Seniors, participants share diet information with each other. In Winnipeg, some residents in a seniors' apartment block who were getting together for coffee began contributing a modest amount to hire a cook who came in to prepare meals for them. In Toronto, a group of seniors took to meeting regularly at a cafe for lunch, followed by a program of films, guest speakers, and craft demonstrations.

As people age and become less active, they generally have diminished appetites and eat less. The quality of the food eaten becomes critical. Malnutrition may be at the root of a variety of problems common to the elderly, including constipation, digestive difficulties, dizziness, falls, brittle bones, confusion, apathy, and disorientation.

Elders who eat poorly do so for many reasons: they can't afford nutritious foods; they don't exercise enough to work up an appetite; they are bothered by ill-fitting dentures; they rely heavily on fast foods because preparing home-cooked meals with the fruit and vegetables needed for a balanced diet is difficult or impossible.

People who are malnourished aren't always thin. Michael Szul tells of a man in his early 80s whose mental capacity was somewhat impaired. "He was slightly plump. You would never have thought he was eating a poor diet. In fact, he was eating a fruit pie a day — that was his staple — and drinking pop. At least he was eating a little fruit, but he was getting no protein." After Szul sent in Meals on Wheels and Homemakers, the patient's mental capacity improved markedly, probably a function of both improved diet and companionship. "Now he knew people cared about him," says Szul.

It is also important to find out what elders drink. They may be drinking too many soft drinks because they can taste the sweetness in them. They may drink more tea or coffee than an aging body can metabolize efficiently. "Even one cup of tea late in the afternoon can cause insomnia that night," says Carolyn Glaze. The solution is a switch to decaffeinated tea or coffee and avoidance of cola drinks, chocolate, and any non-prescription medications that also contain caffeine.

Watch for alcohol abuse. Many elders turn to alcohol as a panacea for aches, pains, and mental distress. Alcohol abuse is common among elders, and is on the increase. If you detect clues of alcohol abuse such as an odor on the breath or bottles stashed around the house, discuss the problem with the elder and encourage him or her to seek professional counselling.

Spacing Meals

Probably the biggest mistake we all make about food is to eat two or three large meals daily. Large meals deposit high levels of glucose and fat into the bloodstream and may slow the flow of blood. Nutritionists now know it is far healthier to eat five or six small meals a day; this places less strain on the digestive system and the heart.

An elderly person (especially one with heart or vascular problems) who is eating two or three large meals a day should shift to this healthier pattern. The shift should be gradual, notes Dr. Alan Huang, a geriatric assessor who is also an assistant professor of medicine at McGill University in Montreal. "It is very hard for people to change dietary habits overnight when they may have lived with their regime for 70 years." Indeed, taking food is one of life's daily rituals, and few of us like to have rituals suddenly overturned.

Another mistake is eating the largest meal in the evening. The morning is when people need the most fuel, to get them started and to sustain them during the day. Ideally, breakfast should provide one quarter of the daily nutritional needs, with the remainder spread among four or five smaller meals.

Getting Enough Fibre

Magazines and newspapers have made the public aware of the importance of eating adequate fibre, once known as "roughage." Among its benefits, fibre helps prevent constipation, a condition prevalent among the elderly. Often they turn to harsh laxatives, not realizing that their constant use over a long period will make the bowel muscles stop working altogether. This habit may also lead to malnutrition: laxatives can prevent the body from absorbing certain vitamins and minerals. A far better solution to the problem is to eat more fibre, increase the intake of liquid (see below), and exercise more.

Good sources of fibre include raw or lightly cooked fruits and vegetables (those the digestive tract can tolerate), hot and cold cereals (preferably those with little or no sugar), and whole grain bread. There are two cautions here. First, a diet's fibre content should be increased gradually. Second, too much fibre may hamper the absorption of nutrients; the family physician can probably recommend adequate levels.

Drinking Enough Liquids

We should all drink the equivalent of six to eight glasses of water a day. This helps keep food moving through the digestive tract. Note the word "equivalent." The daily intake can include tea, coffee, juices, milk and other liquids.

Vitamin and Mineral Supplements

An adequate intake of vitamins and minerals is vital. Many elders are anemic and may need more iron. Some are on medications that deplete the body of certain nutrients. But all nutrients must be properly balanced. Popping pills is not the answer. Consult a professional, who may recommend dietary sources of any missing elements. As Alan Huang points out, many people succumb to advertisements for nutritional supplements that promise a longer, better life. "They stock up on things they don't really need. And there is some danger in taking vitamins and minerals to excess."

Physical Fitness

As a child, this writer recalls members of her grandmother's generation giving advice. "Never run when you can walk," they would say. "Never walk when you can stand. Never stand when you can sit. And never sit when you can lie." The theory, of course, was that the less one used one's body, the longer it would last. Some elders paid dearly. This writer's grandmother spent half her life severely crippled with osteoarthritis.

We now know that this theory was totally wrong. Regular exercise is as important to health as good nutrition, especially with today's labor-saving devices. And we are seeing more and more elders who are in superb physical condition: the 85-year-old woman who teaches yoga at a seniors' club in Victoria; the instructor in her 70s who runs exercise classes at a seniors' centre in Ottawa; and the many older men and women throughout Canada who run in long-distance races.

The Benefits of Exercise

Exercise maintains and strengthens muscles. It also improves digestion, bowel regularity, circulation, posture, joint mobility, and bone strength. It lowers blood pressure and releases nervous tension. It can lift the spirits and help people sleep better. One study showed that those who exercise regularly are four times as likely to survive a heart attack as those who do not.

Exercise also helps improve the appearance. Combined with a good diet, it helps condition the skin and hair and can generally keep people looking far younger — a matter of great importance to the elderly.

As people age, they tend to lose muscle and gain fat. Exercise slows this process. The ability to resist stress also declines; a stress that would cause no alarm reaction in a young person is likely to produce a strong reaction, even exhaustion, in an elder. To a degree, exercise slows this decline as well.

If an older person has never exercised regularly, is it too late to start? Definitely not. One study tracked the progress of a group of inactive elders, including nursing-home residents as old as 96, as they exercised for eight weeks. Their strength increased by as much as 200 percent, their muscles grew in size by up to 15 percent, and their mobility improved dramatically.

What Type of Exercise

No two people are identical, and one person's exercise needs may differ markedly from another's. But generally speaking, geriatricians recommend gentle exercise such as swimming and walking or mildly more strenuous activities such as golf and dancing. Yoga and t'ai chi are gentle forms of exercise that have the added advantage of producing a relaxed state of mind. But for many elders, walking regularly and puttering around the yard and house may be all that's needed.

Personality has a bearing on the exercise chosen. An extrovert will probably enjoy a group activity, perhaps a fitness class. An introvert will more likely enjoy a solitary pursuit such as gardening. Enjoyment is essential. Without it, the exercise will not be relaxing, and an uninterested participant may drop out and stop exercising altogether.

Some activities can be either solitary or group. One such is mall walking — walking in a shopping mall where the ground is level and walkers are protected from the weather. Some people walk in malls on their own, others join clubs. Club members usually walk on Sunday or early in the morning before the stores open and may be accompanied by a fitness instructor.

Getting Started

It is sometimes hard to convince an elderly person of the benefits of exercise, especially if she or he has never exercised regularly. So organized activities should be as convenient as possible — and close to home. An activity that requires no special clothing is probably most appropriate; many pensioners cannot afford the expense of sport clothing and equipment.

Perhaps you or another relative or friend can go along to the first class or mall-walk to provide encouragement and companionship. Often this encouragement is not needed for long. Many elders who join activity programs quickly develop more confidence, a sense of achievement, and a better self-image. And because they feel better both mentally and physically, they become very enthusiastic. They want to keep going!

Elders who have not been exercising regularly should start slowly and increase their ability levels little by little. And those attending weekly classes should allow time for rest and recuperation after the classes.

Emotional Fitness

Discouragement, loneliness, fear, and anxiety can wear down a body as fast as any medical disorder, if not faster. Some emotional problems can be treated only with the help of professionals, and the caregiver may have to decide when the elder needs this help. However, the caregiver and elder can work together to alleviate the circumstances that often lead to emotional problems.

At 97, Myrtle Brodsky is a remarkable elder. She lives in London, Ontario, and took up writing at the age of 80. In a magazine article written when she was in her 90s, she tells of the time she asked a stranger for help crossing the road. He said, "Don't be nervous — we all love you!" and helped her cross. Too often, Brodsky wrote, old people hear a chorus of "Amazing!" and other expressions of admiration. As a result, she continued, "one feels almost as human as a pet dog or cat, but not quite. Now my helper struck the right note — he didn't refer to age or disabilities but just enveloped me in a feeling of being loved — all that any human being can hope for."

The message is clear. Do not parent your parents, treating them as if they were in their second childhood. Their calls for attention may mean simply that they are becoming bored and lonely because you are spending less time with them. The need for companionship is a constant in life.

Alleviating Boredom and Loneliness

It may be necessary to reshape a relationship. This aging person, whether your mother, uncle, or cousin, must now also become your friend. If changing the relationship seems difficult, perhaps you have not been listening to each other. You may be talking *at* instead of *with* one another. Having a good conversation is an art. It means asking open-ended questions: "How do you feel?" for instance, instead of "Are you well?" It means being patient if a reply is not instant; the listener may be carefully formulating a response. It means watching expressions and heeding the tone of voice. It means talking on level ground; you will not have a good talk if you stand towering over someone who is seated or in bed.

When you start to communicate well with older people, you will probably find they have much of interest to say. Those who move more slowly take in more of what is going on around them and often have startling insights.

You and other family members will benefit by taking time to reminisce and learn about family history. Asking such questions as "Who was the woman who always came to tea on Sundays?" may open up a flood of memories — and a treasure chest of information.

Ask about past triumphs; recounting them can help elders come to terms with their lives. And recall funny moments; laughter is good exercise and great medicine. One 107-year-old told a newspaper reporter she owed her longevity to her sense of humor, and she may very well have been right.

Encourage others to visit the elderly; encourage elders to make new friends of all ages. If both halves of an elderly couple are still living, friends are very important; their presence will one day make life easier for the survivor. Again, share the load. If you used to go shopping with an elderly person but now do it by yourself to save time, maybe you can find a friend or relative who enjoys a slow stroll down the aisles. As well, all of your loadsharers do not have to be people. Pets, plants, and music are all therapeutic.

The Active Mind

Mental decline in the elderly is not inevitable. More than 85,000 students, aged 65 and over enrolled in adult education courses in 1984, and many more elders were studying at community colleges and seniors' centres (National Advisory Council on Aging survey).

Younger people, plunging headlong, usually learn faster and often make mistakes. Older people, knowing they must take care if they are not to make mistakes, acquire knowledge more slowly. But one researcher found that more than 50 percent of people aged 81 or older showed no serious decline in reasoning, comprehension, and verbal skills.

The range of activities that elders engage in for their instruction and pleasure is wide. Contact the seniors' group or community centre in your area for more information.

A Communal Approach

For many active elders, support groups are a great way to expand personal horizons and, at the same time, remain very much part of the community. Fully Alive, which started in Calgary, uses senior facilitators to help groups of seniors recognize their potential for growth and their powers to deal with stress, depression, physical changes, and other concerns. The concept has spread to other Alberta communities as well as to Victoria, B.C. In Etobicoke, Ontario, the municipal government has set up a centre where seniors help other seniors solve problems.

Helping others need not be a group activity. Individuals sometimes barter skills. A less active person may cook for a more active neighbor, who in return mows the lawn. Pet sitting and plant watering might be exchanged for housekeeping chores.

Volunteer work is the answer for many elders, particularly if life has been good to them. They may enjoy giving back to society the benefit of their expertise. Agencies value older volunteers for their commitment, maturity, and loyalty. (Some even provide free transportation to the work site.)

Many hospitals and day care centres need surrogate grandparents to work with children. Kids and the elderly often make a great combination, as Torontonian Selma Edelstone discovered when she founded Interlink, a program based on similar programs in the United States. Interlink brings together choirs of seniors and young people for special performances. Edelstone's first project linked the choir of the Baycrest Centre for Geriatric Care with a local school choir. "I'd like to see the concept spread across the country," she says. "It provides a great experience for both the seniors and the youngsters."

When Other Solutions Are Needed

For those elders who are completely housebound, the world can still come knocking at their doors. Quite apart from Meals on Wheels, home helpers, or other social services (see chapter 7), there are many types of home delivery services. If you're thinking about a suitable birthday or other gift for someone, consider ordering his or her favorite meal to be delivered to the home and shared with a friend. Or pay for a series of visits from a hair stylist, manicurist, or massage therapist.

Maybe you and an elder can work out a role to relieve boredom and loneliness. In Hamilton, VON worker Mary Buzzell tells of a woman who felt useless because she couldn't undertake physical activities. "She became the telephone contact for the family. Each day members called in with the news, and she telephoned others to pass it on and collect more. Now she was helping everyone."

However achieved, preventing boredom and loneliness in an elder is critical. To remain active is to enjoy life; to remain involved is to have something to look forward to each morning.

5

Medications

> *The desire to take medicine is perhaps the greatest feature which distinguishes man from animals.*
>
> Sir William Osler

It is hard to imagine the time when people lived in fear of common infections. Most of us now take the existence of the infection fighters, such as penicillin and other antibiotics, for granted. But penicillin was introduced only in 1940, midway in the lives of the elders we know.

The improvements in medications in the last half century have literally changed our lives — mostly for the good. As we saw earlier, many conditions that commonly afflict older people can be managed and controlled by drugs.

However, the elderly are often taking several drugs, and this in itself can lead to problems. Some are due to the drug regime: chances of harmful side effects and interactions between drugs are increased as the drug load increases. Some are due to what doctors call "non-compliance," when an elder does not follow accurately the drug schedule or dosages prescribed. There may be an entirely practical reason for this, such as when poor eyesight causes an elder to reach for the wrong drug container.

Elders and caregivers often do not understand the complexity of the issues here. While there are many excellent publications on the subject (see appendix B), this chapter will present an overview of both the problems and the steps that can be taken to overcome them.

Medication and the Elderly

It has been discovered only recently that many drugs act differently when taken by elders, by the malnourished (which elders often are), or by those with such conditions of aging as atherosclerosis or impaired lung function.

As we grow older, organs such as the liver and kidneys, which are responsible for breaking down many drugs and removing them from the body, do not work as well. Thus it is often difficult to predict precisely *what* effect the drug will have on an elderly patient, or what its side effects will be.

Older people are generally very sensitive to drugs. They seem to experience more side effects (also called adverse reactions), such as mental confusion, dizziness, unsteadiness, and drowsiness.

Unfortunately, most drugs are tested on young people, and dose levels are established for a younger population. This means that drug manufacturers do not know what additional side effects, if any, the drugs will cause in elderly users until the side effects are reported back to them. And that the correct drug doses for older people, especially the very old, are not known.

So, an elder who complains frequently about medications is probably not just making things up. He or she may feel worse, not better, after starting a new medication.

Many older people grew up in an era when one *never* questioned the authority of the person in the white coat. They accept prescriptions without asking questions about the drug they will soon be swallowing. As well, says Diane Dehne, a public health nurse with the Scarborough, Ontario, health department, "They have this perception that if the god, the man in the white coat, doesn't give them a pill, then he is no good."

Elders don't always ask about possible reactions — or report them when they occur. Worse still, they do not provide their doctor with a complete list of the other drugs they take because they may not understand that over-the-counter drugs (OTCs) and even specific foods may interfere with the newly prescribed drug.

A Drug Primer

When drugs are introduced to the market they have two names — a chemical name and a trade name. Acetylsalicylic acid (ASA) is the chemical name; it describes what the drug is. The trade name, like Aspirin, is a catchy word that primarily serves a marketing function.

Once the patent of the original manufacturer has expired, other companies can copy that chemical, have their product tested and approved by the government as the original company did, and market it using its chemical name or another brand name. This will be a generic drug. Apo-Asa is a generic brand of the generic drug acetylsalicylic acid, for instance. Most generic drugs are less expensive than the original brand.

The existence of several drugs on the pharmacy shelf that do essentially the same thing can be confusing to consumers of any age. But elders and their caregivers should be aware of another factor.

Governments and other drug plan insurers that reimburse those over 65 for medications (most provinces do) want to save money on such costs where possible. So if a generic drug comes on the market at a lower cost, the government will direct pharmacists to provide the approved, lower-cost drugs when filling prescriptions. New directives for drug interchangeability are issued regularly.

The patient sees that the drug he or she is taking has changed, but does not know why. The old bottle contained round blue pills, the new one contains oblong yellow ones. Often patients become confused and, consequently, either take no pill at all or take the wrong ones.

Or, the patient may respond differently to the new brand. The effects may be weaker, or stronger, and the side effects may be more pronounced or just different. A common example here is sleeping pills. When they are switched, the elder may complain of not sleeping as well. It may be due to the change of brand or to that person's tolerance to sleeping pills. The user shouldn't merely begin taking more pills, but, rather, discuss the change in effect with the physician.

The table below lists some drugs commonly prescribed to older people, and briefly describes the conditions they treat. The drugs named in the table may also be used for other conditions as determined by the doctor.

Table 5.1 Drugs Prescribed for Common Conditions of Aging

Condition	**Chemical Name of Drug** ***(Brand Name*)***	**Use**
Anxiety	diazepam (*Valium**) lorazepam (*Ativan**)	Some are used to relieve nervousness and tension; others are used in the treatment of insomnia. Also used to help relax muscles or relieve muscle spasm

Condition	**Chemical Name of Drug (*Brand Name**)**	**Use**
Arthritis	flurbiprofen (*Ansaid**) ibuprofen (*Motrin**)	To relieve some symptoms caused by arthritis, such as inflammation, swelling, stiffness, and joint pain. Also used to relieve other kinds of painful conditions
Depression	amitriptyline (*Elavil**) doxepin (*Sinequan**)	To relieve mental depression
Diabetes	glyburide (*Dia eta**)	To reduce the amount of sugar in the blood
Heart condition	captopril (*Capoten**)	To treat congestive heart failure. Also to treat high blood pressure
	digoxin (*Lanoxin**)	To improve the strength and efficiency of the heart and to control the rate and rhythm of the heartbeat
	nifedipine (*Adalat**)	To relax blood vessels and increase the supply of blood and oxygen to the heart. Also used to treat high blood pressure
	nitroglycerin (*Nitrol**)	To treat the symptoms of angina
High blood pressure	hydrochlorothiazide (*Apo-Hydro**)	To treat high blood pressure. Also used as a diuretic (water pill) to help reduce the amount of water in the body by increasing the flow of urine

Condition	**Chemical Name of Drug (*Brand Name**)**	**Use**
High blood pressure (cont'd)	propranolol *(Inderal*)*	To treat high blood pressure. Also used to relieve angina and, in heart attack patients, to help prevent additional heart attacks
Infection	penicillin *(Novopen*)* other antibiotics	To kill bacteria causing infection
Insomnia	diazepam (*Valium**) lorazepam (*Ativan**)	See Anxiety
Parkinson's disease	levodopa *(Lardopa)*	To alleviate the tremors and rigidity associated with Parkinson's disease
Respiratory ailments	theophylline *(Theo-Dur*)*	To treat the symptoms of bronchial asthma, chronic bronchitis, and emphysema. Also to relieve cough, wheezing, and shortness of breath
Thyroid	levothyroxine (*Eltroxin**)	To make up for inadequate hormone production by the thyroid gland
Ulcer	cimetidine (*Tagamet**)	To treat intestinal ulcers and prevent their return. Also used to treat gastric ulcers and some conditions where the stomach produces too much acid

* *There are many brands available. Only one is given here as an example.*

Dealing with Non-Compliance

There are many forms of non-compliance. Mary Buzzell, an official with the Victorian Order of Nurses in Hamilton tells of a retired, well-educated man who began swapping drugs with a group of friends. "One was cortisone, a dangerous drug that needs careful prescribing and careful monitoring by a physician," Buzzell says. "Even if drugs are not dangerous, they should never be swapped."

Another kind of non-compliance is that described by a geriatric assessor — mixing medications in a bowl and just taking a handful when passing by. People who do this have lost track of their complicated medication schedules and so decide to keep no schedule at all.

People who must take several medications a day at different times and according to different instructions sometimes have trouble maintaining the schedule. Here are some tips on how to set up a workable schedule.

- Find several extra containers for the drugs and label them with the times of day when the medicine is supposed to be taken. Fill each container with the correct amount of medicine. Do this for one day (or one week) at a time.

- Set alarm clocks to go off when the medicines are supposed to be taken.

- Keep a chart or calendar near the medicines and list what was taken at what time.

Anyone who forgets to take a medication should call the physician or pharmacist to find out what to do. (Doubling up on doses can be harmful in the case of some drugs.)

Many elders also reduce their intake of drugs that have an unpleasant side effect, or stop taking them altogether. (Patients taking antidepressants, for example, may become constipated and have an unpleasant, dry mouth within days. However, they may not feel the drug's full effect against depression for up to eight weeks.) This form of non-compliance is particularly dangerous. If the patient doesn't discuss the side effects with the doctor or pharmacist, the physician may quite sensibly assume the medication has not worked and prescribe another that has worse side effects.

Drug Reactions and Interactions

Drugs are powerful chemical substances that alter the way the body works. Since no two patients are alike, predicting exactly how someone will react to a drug is difficult. The table below lists just some of the reactions that elderly patients *may* experience when using certain drugs. Many drugs, for example, cause stomach upset if taken on an empty stomach; the problem can be minimized if the drug is taken with food.

In the same vein, there is the problem of drug interactions — when two drugs combine to form an unpredicted and undesirable outcome.

Those taking both a nitrate and a tricyclic antidepressant (the kind most commonly used these days) may experience an excessive drop in blood pressure. Some antidepressants can cancel the beneficial effect of pilocarpine, a prescription eye drop used for glaucoma.

Another interaction problem commonly occurs when prescribed and over-the-counter drugs are taken at the same time. Those taking medications for high blood pressure in combination with a nasal decongestant preparation may experience increased blood pressure. Those on prednisone, an anti-inflammatory drug, who are also taking ASA may start hemorrhaging spontaneously. These combinations should be generally avoided.

Drugs and common foods can also interact. People on prednisone who also drink alcohol run the risk of stomach ulcers. Those on hydroxyzine, a tranquilizer, who consume a lot of coffee, tea, or cola (all rich in caffeine) will find the drug does not have the desired effect.

But how can elders avoid or reduce side effects? By making sure that the doctor knows the names and dosages of the medications being taken, as well as any problems that the elder may have had with drugs. Only then will the doctor be able to find a schedule and dosages that minimize the discomfort.

Information about how the elderly react to drugs is growing. More and more physicians are aware that elders need lower dosages and shorter courses of treatment than younger people. Some are prescribing fewer drugs and scheduling them carefully to avoid interactions. As Winnipeg medical professor and geriatrician, Dr. Colin Powell, says: "Part of the skill is to use drugs selectively. If there are three or four problems, we have to recognize that we can probably treat only one or two, because if we treated them all at once, the person would be rattling with pills."

Table 5.2 Possible Side Effects of Commonly Prescribed Drugs

	Captopril	Diazepam	Digoxin	Doxepin	Flurbiprofen	Gemfibrozil	Glyburide	Hydrochlorothiazide	Levodopa	Levothyroxine	Nifedipine	Nitroglycerin	Penicillin	Propranolol	Theophylline	Warfarin
Appetite loss/gain			•							•						•
Blurred vision			•	•	•				•			•		•		•
Breathlessness	•	•		•	•	•				•	•			•		
Confusion	•	•	•	•	•									•	•	
Depression		•	•		•									•		
Diarrhea	•		•			•	•	•	•	•			•	•	•	•
Dizziness				•		•			•							•
Fatigue	•	•	•		•		•	•	•					•	•	•
Headaches			•		•	•			•	•		•		•	•	•
Insomnia	•	•							•		•			•	•	
Jaundice		•		•	•		•	•						•		•
Joint pain								•						•		•
Muscle cramps						•			•	•					•	
Nausea/vomiting	•		•	•	•	•	•	•	•	•		•	•	•	•	•
Skin rash/hives	•		•	•	•	•	•		•			•		•	•	•
Stomach pain		•			•	•	•	•					•	•	•	•
Swollen legs/feet					•	•					•			•		•
Weight gain					•			•						•		•
Other	•	•	•	•	•	•	•	•	•	•	•	•	•	•	•	•

Strategies for Self-Help

1. *Coordinate with the Family Physician*

The elder should review, with the physician, all medications being used, including over-the-counter (OTC) drugs and vitamin and mineral supplements. Take all the pills and the notes as to how they are being used along to a meeting with the doctor and have them reviewed for instructions. Ask the doctor if any can be discontinued.

2. *Put a Pharmacist on the Team*

Most pharmacists keep computerized files on their customers, and can spot a potential problem instantly when filling prescriptions. It's important that older people find such a pharmacist. If they must have prescriptions filled elsewhere, they should tell the regular pharmacist what additional or new drugs are being taken. The pharmacist should be consulted when purchasing any OTC medication, even if it is only an antacid. It is also helpful for the pharmacist to know what kinds of foods and liquids an elder regularly consumes, and whether she or he has allergies or is a heavy smoker.

Incidentally, elderly people who are planning to travel should take enough of each prescription to last the whole trip. This means supplies will have to be coordinated with the pharmacist well ahead of the departure date.

3. *Keep a Record Book*

If elders do not already do so, they should be encouraged to begin a health notebook. It should indicate the name of the drug and why it is being taken, as well as how and at what time of day drugs are to be taken and when the prescription ends.

If the information is not set out clearly on the drug's label, encourage the elder to question the physician, perhaps with your help, and jot it down. The physician should also volunteer information as to what side effects might be expected. This information, and a description of the side effects the elder experiences, should be noted along with a description of what the drug looks like and if there is any change in appearance when a prescription is refilled.

4. *Respect Expiry Dates*

OTC drugs are required by law to have the expiry date clearly visible on the packaging, and the consumer should check for it. But no expiry date is given on dispensed prescription drugs. The prescription expires when the period for which it is prescribed is ended. For instance, if a month's supply is given it should be used up within that time. If it is not, the drug should be disposed of. A prescription drug may be given for "as needed" use. In this case, patients may keep it for up to six months after it was dispensed, if it is properly stored.

Outdated medications should not be discarded in the garbage, where they may get into the hands of children. Many environmentalists also discourage flushing drugs down the toilet. Your community may collect toxic wastes periodically; if not, check with a local hospital about disposal procedures.

5. *Store Drugs Properly*

Most drugs should be kept in a cool, dry, safe place. This means the bathroom medicine chest is not an ideal storage place — too humid. The kitchen counter or the bedside table are no better. Medications should not be kept in the refrigerator unless this is specified in the instructions. Medicines are best kept in a lockable bedroom closet or in a lockable box in a dresser drawer, where they are protected from sunlight and humidity. Remember, too, to store them well out of the reach of any children who may live in or visit your home.

6. *Take Pills Properly*

Most tablets and capsules should be taken with water. It is important to drink a whole glassful, otherwise the pill may lodge in the esophagus and cause ulceration. When taking a pill while in bed, sit up, drink plenty of water, and remain sitting until the pill has gone right down. When taking liquid preparations, make sure to use the proper measuring spoons, available at your pharmacy. Ordinary kitchen spoons are not accurate enough.

All drugs should be taken according to special instructions. Make sure you understand them; if not, ask the pharmacist.

More Tips on Taking Medications

Here are some hints to make drug-taking and compliance easier.

- When childproof caps, which are now required by law, are hard to open, ask the pharmacist to put the prescription into an easily opened container. Then keep it out of the reach of children.
- When swallowing bitter medicine, hold your nose. When taking tablets that taste bitter, put them on the front of the tongue. The taste buds there detect sweetness while those at the back detect bitterness.
- If dry mouth is a problem, drink a little water before taking pills.
- When putting in eye-drops, try not to blink too much, as this quickly drains them out of the eye. Press gently next to the inner corner of the eye and on the bridge of the nose to prevent quick drainage.

When an Elder's Sight Is Failing

Aging eyes may have trouble reading the small print on labels. If this is the case, the pharmacist will usually supply a label or a separate sheet of instructions in large print.

If the elder has trouble distinguishing colors (commonly blue from green and white from yellow) ask the pharmacist to put pills of different colors but the same size and shape into containers of different sizes, and to identify the drugs clearly on the labels.

If an elder has very poor eyesight, but still perceives colors well, paint the caps of drug containers in different colors — one a vivid blue, another red, perhaps. Wrapping brightly colored tape around the container serves the same purpose. Or, if color perception is not good, cut patches of felt or other heavy material into different shapes and stick them on the containers.

Dispensers - Modern and Old

A daily pill dispenser is helpful for those who must take several drugs. Your pharmacist will show you a selection. Most contain a week's supply of pills.

An alternative practice that was common when our elders were young is to use cardboard egg cartons, writing in big black letters on the top of each carton the name of the pill and instructions as to how to take the medication. This idea for reusing packaging has considerable environmental appeal. In some ways, at least, the bad old days were best.

6

Minimal Care

> *Sometimes very young children can look at the old and a look passes between them conspiratorial, sly and knowing. It's because neither are human to the middling ones.*
>
> Margaret Laurence

Agnes Scott is a public health nurse in Scarborough, Ontario, who both assesses the elderly and gives them homecare. She tells of an 88-year-old woman who was not eating (and whose closest relative was a niece in her 70s with problems of her own). The woman's physician recommended she be put in an institution. Scott went to her home and made a meal. The woman ate it. Scott next ordered up homemaking and meal services. "She just blossomed once she was eating and had regular companionship! But a little later she stopped eating again. She was grieving because the homemaker I had arranged for her had retired. I had to go see her two or three times a week, because she will eat for me. Finally she was eating again. But we have had to change homemakers several times since, and she stops eating each time."

Stories like this are not uncommon. Later life presents a series of losses, and for some people this is accompanied by long periods of mourning. First to go, maybe, are one's own parents; next perhaps, a role — as wage earner or homemaker. Friends die. Often, a spouse dies. Dealing with these losses is one of the greatest challenges to the elderly, and failure to do so successfully may speed their decline.

When an Elder Needs Help

When it is clear an elder needs some assistance in daily living, the decision about the kind of help that is required and who will provide it may fall to you. If so, don't exclude the elder from the decision. "Here you are, perhaps 85 years old, and your daughter and a homecare worker are talking right around you about 'she,' 'her,' and so on as if you weren't there. Well, you'll resent that a lot," says Dorothy Knight, who operates a homecare service in Ontario.

If the elder is capable, let him or her make the decision. "I am very concerned about collusion behind an elder person's back," says Mary Buzzell, director of community education with the Victorian Order of Nurses in Hamilton, Ontario. "Those receiving help must have at least some input into decisions concerning changes in their lives."

Sometimes it is necessary to persuade elders to accept help, whether from you and other family members and friends or from community-based services. Their independence and pride is at stake, so you will have to show they will be no burden by making the help flow two ways. Or, if they won't accept community care because they equate it with welfare, try to persuade them to see themselves as consumers of services to which they have every right.

Homemaking Help

Homemaking help simply means that the elder receives some assistance in keeping the home clean and in repair, as well as in other small chores.

A recently widowed woman moved into a granny flat in her son's backyard. Family members took her out in the car to shop, bank, and so forth, and the grandchildren visited her daily. In return, she would cook or bake for the family. This is a fine example of caregiving as a two-way street. The woman's husband had been very infirm, and she had suffered the loss of her roles as both spouse and caregiver. Had she not taken on the role of part-time cook, she could have ended up feeling useless and depressed.

Other two-way relationships suggest themselves. A granddaughter does the shopping and granddad fixes some lamps needing repairs. A grandson washes a floor, then stays to share a meal grandmother has made.

Food, incidentally, is closely associated with care and nurture. Many old people derive great pleasure from being taken out for a meal or, if they can't get out, from having family members or friends drop by with food and stay to share it.

Public Homecare Services

There has been an amazing growth in both public and private homecare services over the past few years. Among government services, those in Manitoba, Alberta, and Saskatchewan are often cited as the best. Kathy Morpurgo, assistant director of Saskatoon Homecare, tells the story of an 82-year-old client.

"He's been diabetic for 30 years. His wife died about two years ago and his two grown children live in another province. He wasn't doing well. He wasn't eating. His diabetes had worsened; he'd gone from oral medication to injections. His doctor referred him to us, so we sent in an assessor."

The assessor saw an initial need for homecare services and bereavement and general health counseling. An aide began visiting regularly to help the man plan and prepare meals. Initially, she prepared a midday meal for him and left another in the fridge. Soon he began to plan and prepare his own meals.

A nurse also visited him and noted three more needs. He needed foot care, so a podiatrist came in. He needed help for his vision problems, so she set up an appointment with an ophthalmologist. And he needed peer support, so she put him in touch with the local branch of the Canadian Diabetes Association. As well, she taught him how to monitor his own blood-sugar level.

This man remains in the community. And goes out into it: a member of his church takes him grocery shopping. Despite his difficulties, he remains in charge of his own life.

Like many such programs, Saskatoon Homecare is heavily subsidized by government, and clients pay what they can afford, with stated maximums and minimums.

Private Homecare Services

Dorothy Knight, who operates a Selectacare franchise in Oakville, Ontario, despaired when she first went to the home of a client in his middle 80s at the request of his daughter. He and his wife had been drinking for years; she had recently been admitted to hospital with severe cirrhosis of the liver and was not expected to return home. Now he was drinking heavily, getting a neighbor to buy him beer, and not eating.

"I don't think I can offer you much," Knight told the daughter. "He's not going to stop drinking. I can only say to you that we're going to be there every day."

Knight's prediction was wrong. One of her employees was able to get the taciturn man talking by listening to his concerns, and managed to get him to eat. The neighbor was told to stop buying him beer.

"Pretty soon we are going to have him walking around the block," Knight says.

Homecare services provide personal and homecare, shopping and meal preparation, general home management, handyperson help, and transportation for outings, among other services. "We are family substitutes," Knight, formerly a public health nurse, says. "We do what family members would do if they were there."

She tells of one client's family who were amazed when the young woman who had been visiting their elderly relative not only invited the woman to her wedding but arranged for help to get her dressed up and taken to the event.

Companies offer varying degrees of flexibility in their services. Some guarantee a visit at an appointed time by (as often as possible) the same helper. Most will send someone into a home for a minimum of three or four hours; a few will send staff for an hour if that's all that is needed. The fees for these services also vary considerably, but for perhaps $100 a month, an elderly person can get the help you are too busy or stressed to provide. And once you no longer have to rush around doing the chores, and the elder is no longer upset at having to accept your help, you may be able to enjoy your visits more and build a new and better relationship.

Nursing and Specialized Physical Care

Elders who are frail may need help taking baths, changing dressings, or taking medications. They may need foot, skin, and hair care. Family members can usually help with all these — perhaps first learning from a nurse how to change dressings — with one possible exception. No amateur should treat the foot problems of anyone with poor circulation in the feet and legs, since nicks and cuts in the feet of these individuals may not heal well.

If additional help is needed, contact a public or private homemaker service. The Canadian Red Cross Society, for instance, will send in a worker to help the client out of bed, make breakfast, wash and dress the client, give medications, do housework, prepare meals to be eaten later, serve lunch, and help with an exercise routine. Public services call in medical specialists where needed, and most private services do the same or have specialists on staff.

Non-Professional Psychiatric Care

Elders who keep on telling the same tales of long-ago happenings may not be having memory loss. Instead, they may be trying to come to terms with an unsettling experience. And you may be able to help by asking them to elaborate and so reach some further understanding of just what happened. But if they just keep on saying the same thing, the problem may indeed be memory loss.

You may think a wish to talk about dying is a sign of depression and exclaim, "Come on, you've years ahead of you yet!" But this person may just be coming to terms with the inevitable, putting the last odds and ends of life in order, and hence exhibiting a very sound mind. If you sense this is so, hear her or him out, even try to prolong the conversation. For instance, if a wish is expressed for a full scale church funeral, ask, "Do you have favorite hymns you'd like sung?"

Is this person's fear of going out on the streets a trifle paranoid? How safe would you feel if you were somewhat frail, perhaps with diminished eyesight or hearing, and knew criminals might see you as an easy mark? Here, skilled help is available. The RCMP makes presentations to groups and also counsels older individuals on how to avoid becoming a crime statistic.

Professional Psychiatric Care

These days psychiatric care workers will often make home visits to help those with problems. The problem they most often deal with is severe depression.

For those with clinical depression, Marcie Wargon says, "We might prescribe medication, carefully used and carefully monitored." Wargon is coordinator of community psychiatric services for the elderly at Sunnybrook Hospital in Toronto. "Many clients also receive supportive counseling and are encouraged into an activity program," she adds. "If it were a really severe case, we might recommend admission to hospital, but for as short a time as possible."

Innovative Services

An 82-year-old lived alone and didn't know her neighbors. She had been ill for a few days and was weak. While trying to replace a light bulb at the top of her stairs, she fell and broke her hip. That was the end of her independence; she had to be admitted to an institution. "If she'd had a neighbor she could have called on to change the bulb, this would never have happened," says Mary Brown, a liaison officer in Toronto for a new project called Good Neighbors. The idea behind Good Neighbors is simple. Volunteers run a 24-hour answering service. Anyone of any age can call. So can a neighbor who senses something is wrong with another neighbor — perhaps the curtains haven't been opened all day. The volunteer answering the phone calls in the appropriate help — an ambulance service, say, or the health department — or refers the caller on.

"It's getting back to the old neighborhood idea," Brown says. "It starts with saying hello over the back fence or to the person getting into your apartment elevator. It's just a matter of making this the right thing to do again."

As well, there's Telephone Reassurance in Downsview, Ontario. Here a volunteer calls an elder at a set time daily. If there's no reply, or the person sounds distressed, the volunteer gets someone to the home right away to see what's wrong. (You could arrange this kind of program yourself. You, another family member, or a friend or neighbor could be the caller.)

These are just two of the new services available. There are many others.

Where to Turn

To find public home and health care services of all kinds, contact a public health nurse at your local health board. Nurses will come to the home to advise what services and programs are available. They will also give counsel and monitor an aging person's condition, all without charge for those who can't afford to pay. (In some areas, the service is provided only through referral from a physician.)

Community Information Centres (CICs) exist right across Canada in both large and small centres. They provide information on all kinds of services and programs for older people. Some are not called CICs; your public library or health department will know the name of the service in your area. In Quebec, medical and psychiatric help can be obtained through the *Centre Local de Services Communautaires* (CLSC).

Seniors' clubs often have volunteer drivers, and some cab companies reduce rates for older people. If your community has public transit, it may also have a dial-a-bus service that picks up people at home. Organizations such as the Rotary Club and the Royal Canadian Legion help the elderly in many communities by providing free transportation and/or organizing excursions. Ask about all these at the CIC.

Among others, the Alzheimer Society of Canada, the Canadian Diabetes Association, the Canadian Mental Health Association, and the Heart and Stroke Foundation of Canada all help in the organization of support groups. Your CIC or local seniors' centre can probably direct you to support groups in your area.

St. John Ambulance runs courses for those needing to know how to care for old people. Contact your local branch, or the head office at P.O. Box 388, Terminal A, Ottawa, Ontario K1N 8V4. If you need to hire someone to run errands, mow the lawn, go shopping, and so on, advertise on local high-school bulletin boards. Or call the employment centre at your nearest university or college.

The Canadian Red Cross Society runs homemaker programs in many communities. Contact your local branch or the national office at 1800 Alta Vista Drive, Ottawa, Ontario K1G 4J5.

As well as nursing care, the Victorian Order of Nurses offers homemaking, volunteer visiting, foot care, and dietary and other counselling services. In some areas, VON personnel will also cut grass, shovel snow, and take people out by car. Contact your local branch or the head office at 5 Blackburn Avenue, Ottawa, Ontario K1N 8A2.

The Arthritis Society has pool therapy programs, helps patient support groups get started, and in some areas makes home visits. Contact your local branch or the national office at 250 Bloor Street East, Suite 401, Toronto, Ontario M4W 3P3.

As well as games, such as a taped trivia game, the Canadian National Institute for the Blind has talking, braille and large-print books, large-print crosswords, special recording equipment, and craft materials. Among other services, it offers an orientation and mobility service in which clients learn to develop keener senses of hearing, smell, and touch, and to move safely both indoors and out. CNIB volunteers also go into homes to read to clients. Contact your local office or the national head office at 1931 Bayview Avenue, Toronto, Ontario M4G 4C8.

If you live in a large centre, your public library probably has a home delivery service for those who can't get out of the house. Ask at any branch.

To find out more about the RCMP's crime prevention programs, contact your local detachment or write to the Commissioner, RCMP Headquarters, Crime Prevention Branch, 1200 Alta Vista Drive, Ottawa, Ontario K1A 0R2.

To find out if there is a Good Neighbors program in your community, call your local councillor.

7

Making Living Easier

Rest, with nothing else, results in rust.
Wilder Penfield

The elderly woman was distraught. She had recently lost her husband and now, almost overnight, she had lost most of her eyesight. Kathleen Naeyaert, a consultant in gerontology with the Canadian National Institute for the Blind, had come to the woman's home to see how she could be helped.

"We modified her stove by gluing raised markers on the control knobs so she knew what setting she was using," Naeyaert says. "We showed her how to measure and pour foods, how to organize cupboards and clothes, and how to take special precautions. She has audio cassettes and our talking books, and she uses some of our basic aids like magnifiers and writing guides. Today she says, 'Hey, I'm okay! I can do everything. I'm my own boss.'"

There are, in fact, many inventive aids that help the impaired live well. This chapter will look at a few of them. But, as Kathleen Naeyaert did with her client, let's begin by examining some of the simplest ways to make life easier and safer for elders.

Making Everyday Life Easier

Kitchen work can be hard on the back and the feet. A low table or section of counter allows an elder to sit on a chair or stool while preparing food. Standing with one foot on a raised surface can ease back pain; provide a footstool in the kitchen for this purpose, but make sure it can be stored where it won't be tripped over.

For those who have trouble holding kitchen or writing tools, there are several solutions. Thin objects like pens or pencils can be adapted by cutting a hole in a small rubber ball and slipping it onto the gripping surface. Try using the grips from bicycle handle bars on thicker objects. If cutlery presents problems to those with weakened hands, wrap several elastic bands around the handles to make grasping easier.

A pair of tongs to extend the reach can serve many purposes: to get objects from high shelves; to open curtains; to pick up, without bending, objects dropped on the floor; to pull on pants, socks, or stockings when dressing; and to pull up sheets and blankets when in bed.

Velcro clothing fasteners are easier to cope with than buttons or zippers, and footwear with Velcro fastenings is now on the market. So are elastic laces that turn shoes into slip-ons. Shoe repair shops will usually adapt that favorite pair of shoes.

These are just a few ideas. Observing an elder as he or she moves around, and watching for activities that cause problems, will help you come up with many common-sense solutions. And, if you're looking for an appropriate gift, consider one of the following: an electric can opener or mixer for someone with weakened hands; a cordless phone to carry around so its user never has to get up when it rings; an adapter that turns any metallic lamp off and on with just a touch of the hand; a cushioned toilet seat for someone with arthritic or other pains; a device that fits over troublesome doorknobs, converting them into lever-action handles.

Simplifying the Kitchen

Numerous inventive devices make cooking and eating easier. A few of them are shown here.

Extra-grip cutlery has permanently molded handles and comes in shapes suitable for either the left- or right-handed.

Folding stabilizer holds pot steady on stove and stops it from spinning when the contents are stirred. Held in place by rubber suction cups, it folds down for easy storage.

Photo: courtesy Easy Living, Thornhill, Ontario

Making the Bathroom Safer

Those who have trouble standing up after using the toilet, but who still have strong arms, might find a strategically placed grab bar helpful. For those who find the toilet too low for comfortable use, there are devices to raise the level of the seat.

Getting in and out of the bathtub is a common problem. There are many kinds of grab bars, bath seats, and benches. Grab bars must be firmly bolted to a wall; the soap dish type that an elder often grasps for support in the bath is attached only with caulking, and may often break away.

For those who can't get into or out of a tub even with the help of another person, a lifting device may be the answer. Some are cranked manually by the user or a helper; others work hydraulically. Most also support the user in a seated position in the bath.

Removing the Perils of Stairs and Beds

Those with good upper-body strength may need only grab bars and brighter lighting to get up and down stairs safely. For others, a stair lift may be the answer. Several kinds are available, including one that can be installed on a curving staircase.

Grab bars may also be the solution for getting in and out of bed smoothly. If more support is required, a lifting device can assist here, too. Some are powered, others are cranked by hand. Some have a rigid seat, others have a sling.

Standing Up and Getting Around

When getting up from chairs presents problems, grab bars may again be helpful. Alternatively, there is an upholstered armchair whose seat tips up and forward at the touch of a button. The arms tip as well, so the user can hang on to them for added stability while being raised to a standing position. For chairs with hard seats, there is a spring-action padded seat whose upper section rises and tilts forward to help the user stand up. It weighs only seven pounds and can be moved easily from chair to chair.

For help in walking around the home, grab bars, canes, or walkers may do. Other walking aids are available, including one that has three wheels and handlebar grips; downward pressure on the grips brakes the wheels.

This combined walker/shopping cart/seat has rear wheel brakes and folds easily for storage and transport.

Photo: courtesy Able Walker, Burnaby, B.C.

Made of aluminum tubing and cast aluminum, this cane doubles as a seat.

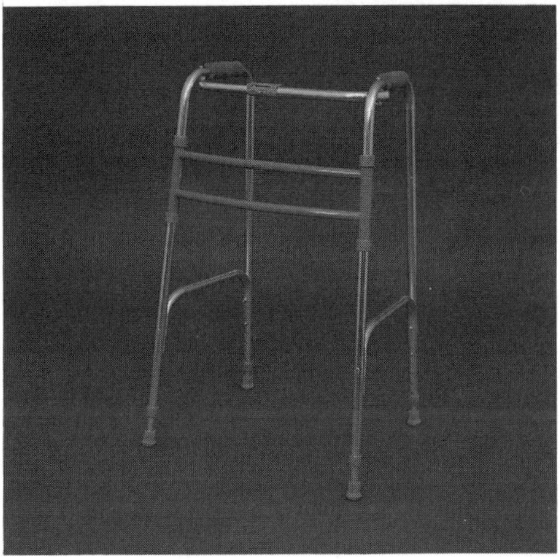

The height of this walker-cum-cane is adjustable and it folds with ease for storage.

Photos: courtesy Doncaster Home Health Care Centre, Unionville, Ont.

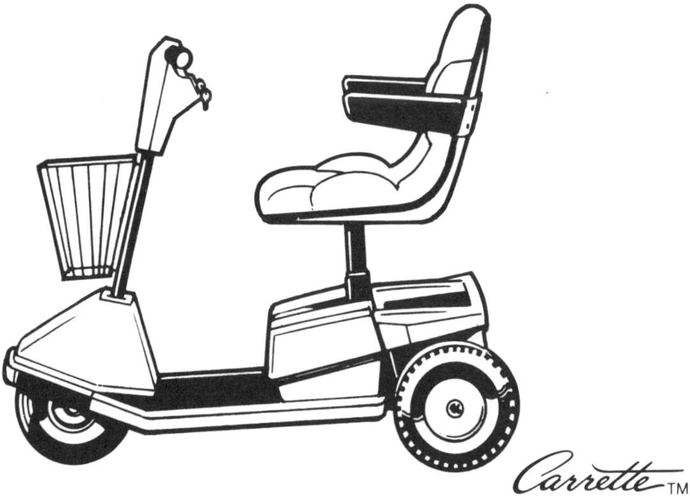

This scooter can travel at more than 8 km per hour, tackle 20 percent inclines and all kinds of terrain, and negotiate doorways because it is only 24 inches wide. Battery-powered, it disassembles into four pieces that fit in the trunk of even a small car.

Sketch: courtesy Everest Jennings, Concord, Ont.

All too often elderly people feel their independence slipping away when they can no longer drive. Many aids are now available to help them stay in the driver's seat longer. One device lets a driver control accelerator, brakes, horn, and headlight dimmer with one hand. Another attaches to the steering wheel to give weakened or painful hands a better grip. Drivers with leg or foot problems will find manual aids to accelerate, brake, change gears, and dim lights. Those who become drowsy while driving will like an alarm that is worn over one ear; it goes off when it senses a head starting to nod or tilt.

Improving Communications

The Medic-Alarm is a small device that has allowed many elders to sleep more soundly and generally live with less fear. An adaption device is added to the user's phone, and he or she wears a pendant around the neck. One quick press of a recessed button on the pendant causes the phone to dial Medic-Alarm's office, where an operator quickly calls the elderly person. If there's no answer, the operator calls a neighbor, ambulance service, and/or relative, whatever the client has requested.

A phone pager may be useful if you're a caregiver who goes out a lot. When the person you care for needs you, he or she dials the number of the pager you carry and it blinks and beeps, warning you to phone or go to him or her.

Bell Canada and other phone companies also have many aids to help those with impaired motion, speech, sight, or hearing use the phone.

Help for the Hard of Hearing

Many aids, other than those that users wear, are available. One translates sounds into sights; for instance, the ring of a doorbell or oven-timer turns on a warning light. Another, a phone/typewriter combination, prints out messages. Yet another is an alarm clock that awakens its user by flashing a strobe light or starting a fan or vibrator.

There are also devices to render sounds from a TV or radio more audible, or to print the words of closed-captioned TV programs as subtitles at the bottom of the screen.

Help for Those with Impaired Vision

Innovative aids now available include talking clocks and calculators; talking and braille watches; a phone that dials a number when the user speaks the name of the person being called; braille typewriters; self-threading darning and sewing machine needles; talking bathroom scales and thermometers; and magnifying glasses that hang around the neck and rest on the chest, leaving both hands free to hold a book, sew, or repair an appliance.

Help for Those with Diabetes

For elderly diabetics who must monitor their blood sugar levels regularly, there are small, efficient monitors. And the lancets and syringes now available for blood samples and insulin injections make the procedures almost painfree. A device for those with poor eyesight makes it easier to measure out doses of insulin. All these devices are small enough to be carried in a purse or pocket.

Help for Those with Incontinence

There are three main categories of aid: absorbent products, external collection devices, and internal collection devices.

In the first category are all kinds of absorbent pads and briefs for both men and women. In the second are products used mostly by men, including drip collectors, little plastic pouches lined with absorbent material, and collection bags which are usually strapped to the inner leg.

The third category consists of catheters, used by both men and women. These are tubes inserted painlessly — provided the procedure is done well — into the mouth of the bladder. Some catheters are for continual use and usually drain into a collection bag. Others are removed after urine is passed. (Many users learn to perform the procedure themselves.)

Encouraging Elderly People to Accept Helpful Devices

Many older people refuse to use aids because they don't want to be seen as having an impairment. One woman who badly needed but refused surgical shoes said indignantly, "They look so terrible!"

The way to encourage an elder to use an aid is to make him or her part of the decision. Carol McPetrie, director of home health care at Shoppers Drug Mart, suggests you accompany the elder to a store selling the needed aid and just let her or him wander around, looking over the various models available and perhaps trying them out. "Very often," McPetrie says, "decisions are being taken out of seniors' hands, and that's not right. Sometimes they just need a bit of encouragement to go and find out what's available."

McPetrie adds that those who refuse to use aids because they look ugly will soon have fewer grounds for doing so. Aids are becoming more attractive and better designed. For instance, grab bars made of strong white plastic instead of cold chromium-plated steel are already on the market, and walkers will soon start appearing with finishes other than institutional chrome.

In the final analysis, however, you may find it impossible to persuade the elder. Mary Buzzell, director of community education with the Victorian Order of Nurses in Hamilton, recalls an experience within her own family. Her aunt, who had very poor sight, was still refusing to use a cane at the age of 90.

"We just had to accept her decision," Buzzell says. "She knew the risks entailed and chose to accept them. She had the *right* to choose. To deprive her of choice would have been to deprive her of her dignity."

Where to Turn

The Canadian Red Cross Society loans devices such as wheelchairs, crutches, and commodes, without charge, for periods of up to three months. For more information, contact your local branch or the national office. Your local department or board of health may also loan wheelchairs and other devices.

Many provinces now have programs to help with the purchase or rental of equipment. Contact your provincial health or social services ministry. If a home must be modified, the municipality will often provide grants; contact your local city hall. When shopping for wheelchairs, bathroom aids, and similar products, look under "Hospital Equipment and Supplies" in the Yellow Pages.

If you can't find the aids you need, try Technical Aids & Services for the Handicapped (TASH) Inc. Its free catalogue describes more than 100 aids not readily available elsewhere. Write to TASH Inc., 70 Gibson Drive, Unit #1, Markham, Ontario L3R 2Z3.

For information on phone service that is appropriate for the elderly, call Bell Canada Special Needs Centre; you'll find a toll-free number under "Customer Service" in the directory. Other Canadian phone companies have similar services.

The Canadian Hearing Society dispenses hearing aids and offers advice on other devices for the hard of hearing. Contact the head office at 271 Spadina Road, Toronto, Ontario M5R 2V3.

The Canadian National Institute for the Blind sells a wide range of devices for the visually impaired. Contact your local office or the national head office at 1931 Bayview Avenue, Toronto, Ontario M4G 4C8.

For aids for those with diabetes, contact the Canadian Diabetes Association, 562 Eglinton Avenue East, Toronto, Ontario M4P 1B9.

8

Daytime Care

When a person is down in the world,
an ounce of help is better than a pound
of preaching.
Edward George Bulwer-Lytton

"I'd say the program has stopped several caregivers from going crazy. Especially those looking after people with severe dementia who can't be left alone: they can't even lie down and have a rest for an hour or so." Mavis Southam, head nurse at the Tache Nursing Centre in Winnipeg, is talking about one of the centre's daytime care programs for elders. More and more such programs are coming into being. They provide part- or full-time care during the day. Some programs fill a predominantly social role, others cater to people with conditions requiring medical supervision.

Regular Day Care

Regular day programs focus on social and recreational activities. "People come in who are tired of looking at four walls," says Rhoda Korstein, day care director at the Baycrest Centre for Geriatric Care in Toronto. One of North America's most extensive centres for elders, Baycrest is probably also the largest institutional provider of elder day care in Canada. The regular program offers arts and crafts, discussion groups, exercises and games. "The clients choose which activities they wish to participate in," Korstein continues. "It's important that they have choices."

Outings are often part of a day care program. Baycrest clients go to plays, and at a Victorian Order of Nurses (VON) centre in Corner Brook, Newfoundland, organises fishing trips in summer.

Many programs also offer some specialized help. For instance, in the centres run by the VON right across Canada, clients can receive foot care and minimal nursing help such as checking blood pressure and monitoring blood sugar levels.

Elders in day programs are usually picked up at their homes in the morning, have lunch at the centre, and are driven home again in the late afternoon. As with other types of daytime care, fees are typically charged on a sliding scale based on the user's ability to pay.

These programs are helping untold numbers of elders and caregivers. In Scarborough, public health nurse Diane Dehne tells of a socially isolated 78-year-old widower who, during one of many falls, broke an arm and cut his head badly. He insisted his knees had just given way, but Dehne found he was taking eight medications as well as alcohol. A geriatrician she called in took him off six drugs but left him on antidepressants because he was still grieving for his wife. The falls stopped right away, and soon after, Dehne persuaded him to enroll in a day care program at a nearby hospital. "He says he's very pleased with it. I think he'll start going to the local seniors' recreation centre soon, and that he'll eventually be off antidepressants."

In Ajax, Ontario, Ada Singh talks of the strains placed on her when her husband Purindra had a stroke four years ago. At first he couldn't speak and she had to do everything for him, as well as doing all the house and garden work. Two years ago, he started to go to day care twice weekly. "It's working well for him," she says. "He's learning a lot there and socializing. He looks forward to going."

Ada Singh is still tired. "It's telling on me. I'm 61 years old. He can take a bath now and walks with a walker, but I have to watch all the time in case he falls." But there's hope for continuing improvement; her husband exercises at the day care centre and now goes to a nearby hospital for physiotherapy. At home, she tries to push him to do a little more all the time. Day care was the start of the comeback for him, and it undoubtedly saved her from becoming totally exhausted.

Specialized Day Care

More and more centres are opening for those who need specialized care for conditions such as Alzheimer, particularly when the disease is in the early stages. "Day care then is a wonderful thing," says Ruth

Mellor, director of communications at the VON national office in Ottawa. "But later on, people with Alzheimer become very confused and upset if you take them out of their homes."

Other types of specialized programs may be available in your area, including physical fitness and swimming programs for people who have Parkinson's or who have had severe strokes.

Day Hospitals

These provide general and specialized medical care to those not needing 24-hour supervision. As with day care, clients come in in the morning and go home in the late afternoon.

Clients of geriatric day hospitals go regularly for checkups or treatment, or irregularly for specialized care such as podiatry, dentistry, otolaryngology (ear, nose, and throat care), or ophthalmology.

"At Baycrest," says Moshe Greengarten, administrator of Resident and Community Services, "many patients come in two or three days a week. When not being examined or treated, they might join a discussion group, do arts and crafts, play cards or bingo, or take part in dance or music therapy programs."

Psychiatric day hospitals function in the same way as their geriatric counterparts. Clients may take part in various types of group therapy, such as movement or occupational therapy.

Day hospitals provide a wide range of services while allowing patients as much independence as they want or can handle. Unfortunately, there are few day hospitals in Canada as yet, but this will no doubt change as public pressure increases and as the population ages.

Respite Care

Simply put, this service is designed to give caregivers a break. All Alzheimer day care programs are really respite programs; as well as providing care to elders, they give caregivers a chance to rest up and live their own lives.

Respite care comes in three forms. Elders can be visited in their homes by professional care providers, travel to a centre or hospital, or go to the home of the professional care provider. Only the first two forms will be discussed here; at time of writing, the third is rare in Canada.

The VON runs a respite program that sends helpers into elders' homes. This is usually the best solution for those severely impaired by Alzheimer, the VON's Ruth Mellor points out.

Services in the home vary from nursing and other assistance to light housekeeping or simply keeping an elder company.

Institutional respite programs are spreading fast. At the Tache Nursing Centre in Winnipeg, which opened its four-bed respite care ward in 1980, head nurse Mavis Southam says, "Most of the nursing homes in Winnipeg now have one bed." Baycrest in Toronto has a respite program, as do several geriatric centres in the Maritimes.

Some elders go in for care perhaps once a year, so their caregivers can go on vacation. Others stay for a few days on a regular basis, perhaps monthly.

Sometimes those in respite care programs are found to have problems that had gone undetected because they were not seeing their physicians regularly. At Tache, for instance, several people coming in for respite care were found to have moderate to severe diabetes needing immediate treatment. On one occasion, an 85-year old who had come in for a stay was incontinent and in need of total care. Staff found her caregivers, a brother and sister also in their 80s, were having health problems of their own as a result of the daily stresses placed on them. The woman had to be admitted to permanent care.

Where to Turn

Your family physician may be able to direct you to appropriate daytime care programs. Or ask at your local community information centre, public health board, seniors' clubs, or public library. You might also contact retirement and nursing homes and chronic care hospitals in your community.

9

Shared or Sheltered Living

> *I find the great thing in this world is not so much where we stand, as in what direction we are moving.*
> Oliver Wendell Holmes

George Towers, 86, has a beautiful four-bedroom home in Toronto but he was getting lonely living there by himself since his wife's death. Besides, he needed help keeping the place up. He went to Sharing, an agency that matches home providers with home seekers. In due course, Gary Higgins moved in. Higgins, 40, arrived with only his duffle bag and his guitar. A gardener, he had been living in a series of $50-a-week rooms. "This is a new and wonderful experience for me, " he says. "We get along just fine."

Towers and Higgins shop together — Higgins has taken over most of the cooking — and play cribbage three or four evenings a week. One cuts the front lawn, the other the back. They have developed a solid relationship. "I'm really enjoying this!" Towers says happily.

For those who can no longer live alone in their own homes because of some disability, and for those who, like George Towers, simply don't want to live alone, many forms of shared or sheltered living exist. Let's take a look at some of the more common and more innovative ones.

Living with the Family

If an elder will be coming to live with you, it's important that the matter be discussed with the whole family — including the kids — and that everyone has a say in what rearrangements of space, duties, and schedules will work best. This is all the more important if the elder is hesitant about moving in and needs to be convinced he or she will not be a burden.

If it appears your work load as caregiver will increase because of the move, talk this over as a family to see how you might get help. Also try to find some appropriate role for the new member of the household, who will most likely want to be involved in what's going on. Perhaps she or he can cook dinner (and the kids can do the dishes) help with garden chores, look after house plants or family pets, or help with shopping.

Garden Suites

These small self-contained houses for the elderly, also called granny flats, will likely grow in popularity, especially in rural and semirural areas where space is not a problem. They are temporary, prefabricated buildings that are dropped onto a foundation in the backyard by crane and winched out again when no longer needed.

Those living in garden suites have as much privacy and independence as they want, while enjoying the security or merely the pleasure of having family members close by.

However, garden suites are clearly not suitable for small inner city lots, and many municipalities have bylaws that forbid putting a second dwelling on a single lot. Despite this, at time of writing, pilot programs are in place in three provinces.

Accessory Apartments

These are small, self-contained suites created in an existing home by rearranging space and, more often than not, installing a second kitchen. Caregivers would typically install suites for elders. Again, many municipalities have bylaws forbidding the creation of this type of housing, but it will probably gain wider acceptance before long.

Renting Out an Apartment

An elder might — bylaws permitting — create a rental apartment in her or his home. It adds to the income flow and, if the tenant is hale and hearty, there's the benefit of knowing someone is around when help is needed or if the homeowner is concerned about security.

Some municipalities will make loans to pay part of the cost of creating new apartments in homes.

Homesharing

George Towers finds his homesharing experience rewarding. But not all such arrangements are successful. Elders are often deeply upset when the sharer moves out. They've lost yet another friend.

Matching services carefully check the credentials of would-be sharers. But many elders are still nervous of having a stranger in the home. Homesharing among friends has a lot to recommend for it. Arranged homesharing appears to work best when people of different generations are matched up.

Congregate Housing

Here, either an older house is converted or a new one specially designed so that several residents have private quarters but share communal spaces (such as dining rooms and lounges) and are provided with main meals. Often, this type of housing is operated by public or non-profit agencies. Individuals also band together to live sharing some expenses.

One form of congregate housing, Abbeyfield Houses, is spreading fast. Residents (usually 10 at most) have either private bed-sitting-rooms or small, self-contained apartments that they furnish themselves. They pay modest fees to cover food, utilities, repairs, mortgage payments, and a housekeeper's salary.

At the time of writing, Abbeyfield has houses in Victoria (two), Kelowna, and Guelph. A third is about to open in Victoria. "Hopefully, at least three more will open in 1990," says Raymond Bosley, president of Abbeyfield Houses Society of Canada at the Toronto head office.

Foster Homes

"Every agency here has them," says Rose Gilbert, clinical head for foster homes at Montreal's Jewish Family Services Social Centre (JFS). She thinks fostering is the best answer for many people who can no longer live in their own homes but don't need nursing care. "Our home managers get very attached to those living with them. We try to get them to give up individuals who will be at risk if they remain in the home, and often they say,'No, if they are going to die, let them die with me.'"

Foster home managers typically look after several elders. They encourage residents to become friends and go out together. Good programs usually have a physician who makes regular visits associated with each home. The JFS program also has a quality-of-life worker who visits with student volunteers. "Some of the youngsters have never talked to an elderly person," Gilbert says. "It gives them a sense of who the elderly are."

Retirement Communities

These come in all shapes and sizes. Villages may have 200 or more dwellings, which may be bungalows, mobile homes, or cottages. Some retirement subdivisions, townhouses, and condominiums provide just a few services — lawn cutting and snow shovelling, for instance. Others provide a full range of services, including homemaking, personal care, and transportation. Some retirement communnities are very expensive; none are cheap. As always, you get what you pay for.

Retirement communities are now starting to provide ongoing assistance for residents who can no longer live independently. Residents reluctant to make yet another move will welcome this security of tenure.

Anyone planning to buy into a retirement community should give the matter careful thought. It may well be possible to sell the house in town, buy a cottage in a rural retirement community, and still have cash left over. But money isn't the only security in life. Friends, acquaintances, the doctor, dentist, and other professionals who have given service over the years — even staff in stores and banks — represent security. And the sense of loss when they're no longer part of the elder's life may be greater than was anticipated.

But some people go into retirement communities expecting to hate them, and find they thoroughly enjoy themselves. Margaret Byers, 77, decided several years ago that she and her husband had to go into a retirement community because neither was in good health. They chose Northwoodcare in Halifax. "I was really reluctant," she recalls. "I said I wasn't going to take part in any activities." Today, the recently widowed Byers says, "This is a wonderful place to be, let me tell you. I do any volunteer work I can. Soon after we came here, my son said he'd have to get a beeper to find out where I was!"

Retirement Apartments

These rental units are often operated by government or non-profit agencies and hence are available at low cost. As with retirement communities, the level of services varies.

Some retirement apartments are imaginatively located. Sokol Manor in Brandon, Manitoba, shares a building with an elementary school. The 32-unit apartment section is separated from the school by a glass-walled lounge, but children and residents can meet to chat, and the children put on little shows for special occasions such as Hallowe'en. They also enjoy practising their reading skills on the residents.

Apartments are also starting to be linked to shopping malls so residents can shop without going outdoors. There are several in Winnipeg, among them Kiwanis Place and Fred Douglas Lodge.

The Wellesley Retirement Group, headquartered in Winnipeg, is setting up many apartments. By the beginning of 1990 there will be Wellesley apartments in Winnipeg, Victoria, Montreal, and Hamilton, and over the next few years the company plans to open another four or five.

Life-Care Communities

Also called life-lease communities, life-care communities are usually high rises. In exchange for a substantial entry fee and monthly fees thereafter, residents are guaranteed that they will receive increased levels of medical care and other services as needed, often without additional fees. Even in these communities, however, those who become very infirm may be moved to hospital. Anyone contemplating this form of housing should find out if the entry fee is fully or partially refundable. It often is. For instance, at the Kiwanis Lodge in Winnipeg, it is fully refundable, while at the Hesperus Fellowship Community in Vaughan, Ontario, those who leave get partial refunds that decline with each year spent in the community.

Continuing Care Retirement Communities (CCRCs)

These comprise not one but a cluster of facilities and come in two forms. In the first, all facilities are located on one campus, as is the case with the Baycrest Centre for Geriatric Care in Toronto. On its grounds are a minimal care apartment residence, a recreation complex, a home for the aged, and a chronic care hospital. Those coming into such facilities are thus guaranteed they will never have to make another disruptive move unless by choice. The Northwoodcare complex in Halifax is another example of this type of CCRC.

The other type also has multilevel care facilities but not on one campus. The municipality of Niagara, Ontario, runs a system of long-term care facilities that links nursing and retirement homes, group homes, recreational and health care centres, and so forth. According to Doug Rapelje, director of the region's senior citizen's department, the overall focus of the whole multi-level care system is to "recognize the potential rather than the limitations of old people."

This is a thought that cannot be overstated: concentrate on what an aging person *can* do, not on what he or she cannot do.

When It's Time for a Change

Any change in living arrangements should be thought through extremely carefully beforehand. The elder you care for may find it helpful to answer the questions below. By the end of the exercise, she or he will have a clearer view of how appropriate (or inappropriate) the proposed change is.

Some questions are more important than others. The first four are key; they far outweigh considerations about spending more on public transit, for instance. And some responses will almost certainly be negative. As Norman Blackie, executive director of the Canadian Association on Gerontology, points out, this will almost certainly be a time of trade-offs; for instance, to gain more security, this person may have to accept smaller living quarters. Some questions may simply not apply in this person's case; she or he should just skip them.

- Will the arrangement still suit me 5 or 10 years hence?
- If not, how disruptive might I find another move?
- How confident am I that I won't have to move again in the foreseeable future unless I choose to do so?
- How important is privacy to me?
- Am I the kind of person who likes routines?
- Am I generally gregarious or more of a loner?
- Might I feel confined if I have to live in smaller quarters than I currently occupy?
- Will this living arrangement still be affordable 5 or 10 years hence?
- And will the survivor be able to afford it?
- How important is it to me to have a house to leave to someone in my will?

- Will it mean I'll have to spend more money on such things as transportation and long-distance calls to keep in touch with family and friends?

- If I'm going into this arrangement with another person, how suitable will it be for the survivor if one dies?

- Will I have plenty of opportunity to keep up my hobbies and recreational activities?

- Have I, overall, given sufficient thought to the course of action I am proposing to take?

If the answer to the last question is "No," try drawing a line down the centre of a sheet of paper, on one side writing the reasons this would be a good move, on the other the reasons it would be a bad one.

You, the caregiver, should also think about the effect the proposed change would have on your life. Your elder's wishes should come first, but if, for instance, you'd have to drive twice as far and hence couldn't visit as often as you do now, it's only fair to point this out.

Look Before You Leap

Those planning to make a change in living arrangements should ask for a trial visit, especially if the move would mean selling their present home.

Those who have recently lost their spouses and want to move to combat loneliness or grief should put off a decision to move. Any decision made when one is grieving may be regretted. Instead of moving, encourage the one who has been widowed to take in a home-sharer temporarily or visit friends or take a vacation.

Many seniors' complexes have waiting lists. So it makes good sense for elders to tour several, make a choice, and get their names on the waiting lists. George Towers had to wait a while before Sharing matched him with Gary Higgins. But for both men, planning in advance and being prepared to wait has paid off. Higgins says, "In earlier generations we had our grandparents around. We didn't ship them off to homes." He is clearly delighted that Towers hasn't been "shipped off" and Towers clearly delights in his friendship.

Where to Turn

The family physician may be able to direct you to various forms of shared and sheltered living available locally. Or ask at your community information centre or *Centre Local de Services Communautaires*. Or contact the local housing authority, public health board, provincial senior citizens' ministry, or local office of the Canada Mortgage and Housing Corporation. Golden Age or other seniors' clubs may also be able to help, or look in the Yellow Pages under "Retirement Communities and Homes".

10

A Home Away from Home

In human life there is constant change of fortune
and it is unreasonable to expect an exemption
from the common fate.
Plutarch

Most elderly people do not want to go into permanent care, but the time may come when physical disabilities and fatigue, combined with fear of becoming a burden to others, make such a move necessary. A few even welcome the change, especially if they will be joining friends already at the facility.

When the time is right to find that home away from home, the caregiver must help ensure that it will be a *good* home and that the elder is supported during the transition period. No one accepts the loss of independence without some pain.

There are ways to ease the distress, as you will discover. Perhaps the most important is ensuring this person (if she or he is capable) takes part not only in the decision to move, but also in the choice of home. Teamwork now will make the move easier on both the elder and the caregiver.

What to Look for

The physician will be able to suggest the type of facility that is most appropriate, depending on the level of care the elder needs. Here's a rundown of the various types.

Retirement homes or lodges — also called rest homes, senior citizens' homes, or personal-care homes — provide accommodation, meals, and a range of activities. They are generally privately operated, and the residents pay full fees. While they may offer a little nursing care such as help with medications and bathing, they do not provide extensive health care.

Homes for the aged typically subdivide into two categories: residential homes provide health care and personal assistance for less than two hours a day, and extended-care homes are for those who need more attention. Fees charged depend on whether the home is private or non-profit (operated by some level of government, a charity, or a community service organization).

Nursing homes provide more nursing care than homes for the aged. Again, they may be private or non-profit.

Chronic care hospitals are for those who need regular medical assistance and ongoing nursing care. They may also be private or non-profit.

If your area offers the luxury of choice, the two of you should visit at least three homes before deciding which will be the most suitable. Do as much research as you can, by questioning staff members and residents, as well as people in the community who have contacts with the home.

The worksheet entitled "Choosing the Right Home" in appendix A will help you compile this research and compare homes under consideration. The whole process will take several days, if not weeks. Allow time for this and for thorough discussion of your findings with *all* concerned.

When assessing location, consider who will visit most often. If you will be doing so, then a home near you will be most suitable. If the elder is fond of grandchildren who enjoy visiting, or has good friends in the community, a location close to them may be best.

As far as safety is concerned, you're looking for such things as an adequate distribution of grab bars, the absence of highly polished floors with rugs on them, and elevator doors that close slowly. As for recreational facilities, look for exercise areas and equipment, facilities for physical activities such as yoga or dancing, or games such as lawn bowling. When checking entertainment facilities, look for board and card games, books, TVs, VCRs, and radios.

When asking about staff qualifications, bear in mind the comment made by one nursing home operator: "All the qualifications in the world aren't worth a toot if the staff are not caring, compassionate people who enjoy working with the residents." So by all means ask about qualifications, but also look for signs of empathy between staff members and residents. As you study the relationship between them, look for staff members who address residents by first name and who do not raise their voices when talking to residents who hear perfectly well.

Try to find out if staff are visible at all times, and thus, if help is right at hand when a resident has a problem.

As for the residents' general state of mind, look for signs that the person you have been caring for will fit in. If, for instance, many of the residents are victims of Alzheimer and have dementia, while he or she does not, this is not the right place.

When assessing the residents' physical condition, look for cleanliness of person, hair and clothing, and examine the condition of people's clothes and footwear.

Many homes have residents' councils these days. That's an excellent sign. Some have both councils and a joint residents/staff committee. One such is Pioneer Lodge in Salmon Arm, B.C. Kathleen Dalkey, 85, is the council's recording secretary, a position she has held since she went into the home in 1983. The council has been instrumental in improving the way the home is run, and it also organizes charitable ventures. Dalkey explains: "We raised money to build a ramp for a little girl who's in a wheelchair. We sent out hampers. We sent a table and four chairs to the women's emergency shelter. My goodness, we do all kinds of things!"

Dalkey, who was born in a sod-roof house built into a hillside in Saskatchewan, and who once was a schoolteacher, has good advice for anyone who must go into a home: "Don't worry about what you have behind you. Look to what is ahead."

Making a Trial Visit

Once the facility has been chosen, the elder should, if possible, make a trial visit before moving into permanent care. All too often, people sell their homes and move, *then* find they don't like the new arrangement. Elisabeth ("Hoppy") Hopkins is an example. When she was in her late 70s she had a bad fall and decided to sell her home on Galiano Island, B.C., and go into care. Within months, she had checked herself out and was living in a rented cottage. "It was an awful enclosed feeling," she said later. "They were extremely nice people. But I missed all my young friends." Now 95, she still lives by herself. She has three hours a week of homecare and is also helped and sustained by a group of friends and neighbors. "People are so good to me," she says.

Making the Move

An administrator at an extended-care facility in the Maritimes talks with profound compassion about how her new charges feel the day they are admitted into permanent care. "This is an overwhelming experience for them. They are probably contemplating all the losses they're suddenly experiencing."

It is, more often than not, an extremely sad day. How would you feel if, at one fell swoop, you lost your home and possibly your community, your freedom to come and go as you please and to make such simple choices as when and what to eat?

For you the caregiver, the sadness will also come from the feeling of diminishment in having admitted you could no longer cope.

To make it all easier, then, come with the person on the first day and stay for several hours. New residents may not recall all they are told because they feel overwhelmed. Help get them settled. Remind the elder that, yes, this is your closet here, and lunch is at 12 o'clock in the dining room just down the hall. Escort the elder to the dining room. If you are not allowed to have lunch there yourself, be there to visit in the afternoon.

In many facilities, social workers or registered nurses assess some of the new residents' needs, so that if the bedroom is to be shared, a smoker won't be put with a non-smoker, or an avid TV watcher with one who prefers to read. If this has not been done, here is another role for you.

Talk to staff, preferably in the elderly person's presence. Explain, for example, that your mother is not too gregarious but loves reading, so she'd really rather stay in her room with a good book than go to the lounge to play bridge. Tell her nurse that she has a great sense of humor and enjoys a good laugh — or that she's rather a serious person and likes a good discussion. These staff members are going to be sharing the caregiving role with you from now on, and they need to become familiar with the elder's likes and dislikes.

One last point. Never, never lie. Never say this is a visit when it's an admission. "Some people who have been lied to have refused to stay," says the administrator. "They have that option."

The Days that Follow

Make sure you develop a definite pattern for continued contacts. In other words, don't be unrealistic and start a routine of visits you can't keep up.

Much depends on your prior relationship. If you were close and saw each other on a regular basis, that should continue. But if this will mean hardship to you, be honest and say so. Maybe you could visit every Saturday, and a brother or sister every Sunday. Or maybe you could visit twice a week and phone on the days in between.

Distress over the loss of freedom lasts an average of six months. "But some never adjust," the compassionate administrator says. "You simply have to accept that. The totally private person who has always lived alone may find communal living extremely hard."

While some relationships deteriorate after admission — mostly because elders have not been part of the decision and feel they were "put away" — the majority *improve.* "The stresses of caregiving are largely lifted. And the elder will stop feeling guilty about being a burden. Communications improve, and the elder and caregiver get back to a healthier relationship. That is very good to see."

Where to Turn

To find extended-care homes of various kinds, ask the family physician, write to or call the local health board, or drop in at your community information centre or *Centre Local de Services Communautaires.* Staff at public libraries can also direct you to listings of homes. As well, many libraries' reference sections have two comprehensive guides published by the Canadian Hospital Association: *Directory of Long-term Care Centres in Canada* and *Canadian Hospital Directory.* Both are updated annually.

11

Peace of Mind

> *To grow old is already a privilege of Providence in itself, and that is why life will always be for me an indestructible treasure from birth to a natural death.*
>
> Dr. (now senator) Paul David, founder of the Montreal Heart Institute.

Thinking about and planning for one's own death — or for that of the elderly person you have cared for and loved — is not one of life's pleasant tasks. But elders and caregivers alike should make efforts to prepare for the event. Elders should set down clear instructions as to financial and legal matters. When they cannot manage their affairs, caregivers must step in and help, or see that the appropriate counsellors are engaged.

Insurance

First, be sure that any private medical insurance is fully paid up and that you know exactly what it covers. Life insurance should be reviewed to make sure it is appropriate. (Incidentally, if a life insurance policy names a beneficiary, funds will go immediately to that beneficiary without being subject to probate, taxation, and possible claims by creditors.)

Pensions, Annuities, and Registered Retirement Income Funds

It is important to know what income pensions, annuities, and Registered Retirement Income Funds are providing in the way of income now, and what will happen to payments upon death.

Power of Attorney

When you grant power of attorney, you give the person or persons named the right to manage your affairs, financial and otherwise. A restricted power of attorney gives those named the right to manage only those affairs set out in the document. Either document is drawn up by a lawyer or, in Quebec, a notary; they are relatively simple, so fees will not be high.

Wills

Both elders and caregivers should have wills. If a person dies intestate (without a will), the Public Trustee or, in Quebec, the Public Curator will step in, determine how the assets are to be divided among relatives, and charge quite heavy fees for winding up the estate.

Wills are usually drawn up by a lawyer or, in Quebec, a notary. The fee will be relatively small unless the estate is large and bequests are complex. Handwritten wills, duly signed and dated, are also acceptable but best used in very straightforward circumstances. For example, "I, Sarah Doherty, leave everything to my only son, Adam Doherty."

Since wills are valid only if those making them are individuals of sound mind at the time, it is important that they be written before severe mental disabilities set in.

Among other things, a will names the executor(s) (the person or persons who will handle the estate), directs the payment of any debts or taxes, and names those people who will benefit and to what degree.

When drafting a will, think of the here and now. This is what you would like done if you were to die tomorrow. But circumstances change, so the will should be reviewed every three years or so. If changes are in order, it may not be necessary to make a whole new will. Fairly minor changes in bequests can simply be listed in a letter to the executor(s).

Living Wills

A living will is a statement attesting that the person signing it does not want medical personnel to take heroic measures or use artificial means to prolong life. It can be handwritten, without the participation of a lawyer. Two witnesses, who will later be able to testify that the person who drew up the will was of sound mind at the time must co-sign it.

If you are caring for someone who often talks about dying and no longer enjoys life, you might suggest that this is the time to make a living will.

Funeral Arrangements

When drawing up a will, the elder should state what funeral arrangements are preferred, if any, and whether the body is to be buried or cremated, or donated to medical research.

It is really important that the caregiver and elder think through and set down in writing somewhere what should be done in the event of death. For those who remain, a death is inevitably upsetting, even when it frees someone from pain. The world shrinks away a little, and for a while it may seem as if your centre cannot hold. It is so much easier for you, the caregiver, if all the arrangements have been planned in advance and need only be carried out.

In Case of Death

Normally, when someone dies at home, you call either an ambulance or the family physician. If you call an ambulance, and the attendants determine there are no vital signs, they will call a doctor or coroner to pronounce that this person is no longer alive.

If there is to be a funeral, a family member or the physician calls the chosen funeral home. From here on, the funeral director takes over, if that is what you wish. He or she will arrange for all the documentation necessary, call to make arrangements for the service itself, and provide flowers and cars. If the person is to be buried, and if a cemetery plot has not been bought in advance (many are), the funeral director can arrange this purchase too.

Funerals can also be bought in advance. The money you pay goes into a trust fund, and the interest it earns compensates the funeral director if costs rise.

Memorial societies, whose members pay a small lifetime fee up front, offer inexpensive alternatives. They work through funeral homes, but the body is not embalmed, coffins are plain, and memorial services, if required, are simple. Typically, all this reduces costs by about half to one third. Memorial society costs can also be prepaid.

If there is to be no funeral, the family or the physician still calls a funeral home. For a relatively small amount, it will furnish an appropriate casket, depending on whether there will be a cremation or a burial, and also provide transportation to the crematorium or cemetery. Once again, the funeral director can handle all documentation. Alternatively, a family member can obtain the documents required from the coroner or the family practitioner. He or she completes these documents which the crematorium or cemetery will need.

These days, many people prefer that those left behind make donations to medical or other charitable organizations rather than buying flowers or wreaths. This is a practice that should be encouraged. Flowers also die, while good works endure.

As we wrote at the start of this book, many of today's elders have survived huge societal and scientific change, and survived unscathed. They are often full of wisdom, often full of wit. In researching the book, it has been our pleasure to talk with many dedicated people who have made careers of helping elders and who do so with the respect and compassion those elders deserve. We hope that by sharing with you, the caregiver, some of their accumulated wisdom and experience, we have been helpful to you in the vital role you have assumed. If so, we are doubly rewarded.

Appendix A

Worksheets

WORKSHEET 1: POTENTIAL CAREGIVER

Circle your responses on the page or write them on a separate sheet.

1. I intend to help this elder out of:
   loyalty
   love
   duty
   necessity

2. Our relationship is:
   excellent
   good
   fair
   poor
   largely non-existent

3. I believe this elder
   loves me
   likes me
   respects me
   is indifferent toward me

4. I think she or he will accept my help
   willingly
   begrudgingly
   not at all

5. I find set routines and repetitive tasks are:
   enjoyable
   not enjoyable

6. My perception is that this elder needs my help in the following ways: ....
   ....

7. My own physical health is:
   excellent
   good
   fair
   poor

8. More often than not my state of mind is:
   excellent
   fairly good
   poor

9. I suffer from stress, anxiety, and/or depression:
   never
   rarely
   often

10. At present the amount of free time I have is:
    abundant
    limited
    minimal

11. My answer to the previous question will:
    change in the foreseeable future
    not change in the foreseeable future

12. Can I count on others, be they relatives, friends, or neighbors, to share the caregiving role with me?
    Yes
    No

13. Will assuming the caregiver role for this elder imperil my function as wage earner and/or caregiver to others?
    Yes
    No

14. Is there another person who might be a more appropriate caregiver than me?
    Yes
    No

15. If your answer to the previous question was yes, name the person and explain your reasoning.
    ....
    ....

WORKSHEET 2: ELDER

If the elder has difficulty seeing or writing, it may be a good idea to enlist the help of a third person to read out the questions and write the responses. This will ensure the elder's privacy and encourage his or her honest self-examination.

1. My relationship with this potential caregiver is:
   - excellent
   - good
   - fair
   - largely non-existent

2. I believe I shall accept her or his help:
   - willingly
   - unwillingly

3. Should my prime caregiver be another family member, friend, or neighbor?
   - Yes
   - No

4. If your last answer was yes, who is the person you would prefer, and why?

   ....

   ....

5. Would I prefer to be looked after by professional health care workers?
   - Yes
   - No

6. How willing am I to accept help?
   - very
   - somewhat
   - not at all

7. Right now I need help in the following ways:

   light housekeeping
   laundry
   heavy housekeeping
   meal preparation
   home maintenance
   yard chores
   dressing
   bathing
   taking the right drugs
   managing finances
   other (specify)...

8. Do I expect I shall soon need help in more ways?

   Yes
   No

9. My prime concerns are:

   my physical well-being
   my emotional state
   my financial security
   fear of being mugged or robbed
   other (specify)...
   ....

10. Do I always tell others, including my doctor, the true state of my health?

    Yes
    No

11. Does it seem to me that I am becoming more contented and mellow as I grow older?

    Yes
    No

WORKSHEET 3: CHOOSING THE RIGHT HOME

Because chapter 10 explains what aspects of a long-term care facility to look at when compiling these ratings, read the chapter before completing this worksheet.

Make two copies of the worksheet for every home under consideration. The caregiver fills out one copy, the elder the other. Rate each home by checking the appropriate column on the right. Then use your findings as a basis for comparing and discussing. Don't merely select the home with the highest number of Excellents and Very goods because some factors will be more important than others; for instance, a no-pets-allowed policy will be of no concern to someone who was never a pet lover.

Institution:	Excellent	Very Good	Good	Fair	Poor
The location is					
Condition of exterior and grounds is					
General condition of interior is					
Bedroom arrangements are					
Bathroom facilities are					
Preparation and appearance of meals are					
Entertainment facilities are					
Occupational facilities are					
The ratio of staff to residents is					
Qualifications required of staff are					
Relationships between staff and residents appear to be					

	Excellent	Very Good	Good	Fair	Poor
Visibility of staff in residence is					
Residents' ability to choose their rooms and roommates is					
Residents' ability to bring in their own furniture, photos, etc., is					
Freedom for pets to visit or live in facility is					
The state of mind of the majority of residents appears to be					
The physical condition of the majority of residents appears to be					
Social interaction among residents appears to be					
Residents' responses to my/our questions were					
The ability of residents to participate in how this facility is run seems					
The availability of pastoral care support here seems					
The availability of palliative care for those who are dying is					
The reputation of this facility generally is					
My/our ability to pay the fees now and in the future is					
My overall opinion of this facility is					

Appendix B

Sources

This list of recommended reading and viewing materials is by no means exhaustive. More and more publications and videos on various aspects of aging and caregiving are coming onto the market, and a comprehensive list would have taken up far more space than is available.

Note that only the head office cities of various organizations are listed. Many organizations, such as Health and Welfare Canada and the Canadian National Institute for the Blind, provide materials through the local or regional branch. And, as always, your nearest public library is a valuable resource centre for these and other materials.

GENERAL READING AND VIEWING

Dychtwald, Ken and Joe Flower. *Age Wave: The Challenges and Opportunities of an Aging North America.* Jeremy P. Tarcher, Inc., 1989.

Expression. Quarterly newsletter of the National Advisory Council on Aging, Ottawa.

Extra Mile, The. Video from Pioneer Lodge, Salmon Arm, B.C.

Good Times. Monthly magazine. Good Times, Toronto.

Gordon, Dr. Michael. *Old Enough to Feel Better: A Medical Guide for Seniors.* Seal Books,1987.

Novak, Dr. Mark. *Successful Aging: The Myths, Realities and Future of Aging in Canada.* Penguin Books Canada Ltd., 1985.

Senior Times, The. Twice-monthly newspaper. Publications Newborn Inc., Montreal.

Something to Celebrate. National Film Board video No. C 0183 023.

Today's Seniors. Monthly newspaper. Metroland Printing, Publishing and Distributing, Mississauga, Ont.

Underwood, Richard D. and Brenda Breeden Underwood. *Wise & Healthy Living: A Commonsense Approach for Aging Well.* Self-Counsel Press, 1989.

Wigdor, Blossom, with Arthur Drache. *Planning Your Retirement: The Complete Self-Help Guide.* Grosvenor House Press Inc., 1987.

Wigdor, Blossom and David K. Foot. *The Over-Forty Society: Issues for Canada's Aging Population.* James Lorimer & Co., 1988.

PHYSICAL PROBLEMS

Alzheimer's Disease: A Family Information Handbook. Health and Welfare Canada, Ottawa.

Arthritis News. Quarterly magazine. Arthritis Society, Toronto. (Also a French Version, *Communiqué.*)

Crawford, Irene. *Aids to Independence: A Guide to Products for the Disabled and Elderly.* International Self-Counsel Press, 1985.

Davy, Cindy and Gillian Parker. *Exercising With Arthritis: Stretching And Strengthening Exercises For Canadians With Arthritis.* Trelle Enterprises Inc.

Diabetes Dialogue. Quarterly magazine. Canadian Diabetes Association, Toronto.

Gartley, Cheryle B. (editor). *Managing Incontinence: A Guide to Living with Loss of Bladder Control.* Jameson Books Inc., 1985.

Housing and Support Services for Physically Disabled Persons in Canada. Handbook and sourcebook. Canadian Rehabilitation Council for the Disabled, Toronto.

Informer, The. Newsletter of the Simon Foundation of Canada, Tecumseh, Ont.

Living With Vision Loss. Video. Canadian National Institute for the Blind, Toronto.

Lyons, Walter. *Coping and Helping with Alzheimer's Disease.* National Advisory Council on Aging, Ottawa.

Mace, Nancy L. and Peter V. Rabins. *The 36-Hour Day: A Family Guide to Caring for Persons with Alzheimer's Disease, Related Illnesses, and Memory Loss in Later Life.* Warner Brooks, 1989.

Reflections on Suffering. National Film Board video No. C 0182 048.

Schiff, Myra and Lori Kociol. *Alzheimer: A Canadian Resource Guide.* McGraw Hill-Ryerson Ltd., 1989.

Vehicles and Adaptive Aids for Elderly and Disabled Drivers: A Buyer's Guide. Canadian Government Publishing Centre, Ottawa.

Visage. Quarterly newsletter on aging and vision loss. Canadian National Institute for the Blind, Toronto.

PSYCHOLOGICAL PROBLEMS

Forbes Home, The. National Film Board video No. C 0182 084.

It's Just Your Nerves. Pamphlet. Health and Welfare Canada, Ottawa.

Mental Health in Later Years. Booklet. Health and Welfare Canada, Ottawa.

MEDICATIONS

Griffith, H. Winter. *Complete Guide to Prescription & Non-Prescrition Drugs' Side Effects, Warnings and Vital Data for Safe Use.* The Body Press, 1989.

Berner, Mark S. and Gerald N. Rottenberg (Editors). *Guide to Over-the-Counter and Prescription Drugs.* Canadian Medical Association, Ottawa, 1990.

Smith, Dorothy L. *Understanding Canadian Prescription Drugs: A Consumer's Guide to Correct Use.* Key Porter Books, 1989.

Using Medicine Safely. Booklet. Saskatchewan Health, Regina, Sask.

Wolfe, Sidney M., Lisa Fugate, Elizabeth P. Hulstrand, Laurie E. Kamimoto, and the Public Citizen Health Research Group. *Worst Pills Best Pills: The Older Adult's Guide to Avoiding Drug-Induced Death or Illness.* Public Citizen Health Research Group, 1988.

CAREGIVERS' GUIDES

Last Days of Living, The. National Film Board video No. C 0185 112.

MacLean, Helene. *Caring for Your Parents: A Sourcebook of Options and Solutions for Both Generations.* Doubleday, 1987.

Marge, the Blamer and How to Help Her. Video. Canadian Learning Co., Scarborough, Ont.

My Mother, My Father. Video. Canadian Learning Co., Scarborough, Ont.

Priory, the Only Home I've Got. National Film Board video No. C 0178 193.

Thompson, Wendy. *Aging is a Family Affair: A Guide to Quality Visiting, Long-term Care Facilities and You.* NC Press Ltd., 1988.

Time for Caring, A. National Film Board video No. C 0182 045.

NUTRITION

Brody, Jane E. *Jane Brody's Nutrition Book.* Bantam, 1987.

Canada's Food Guide Handbook. Health and Welfare Canada, Ottawa.

Food Additive Pocket Dictionary. Booklet. Health and Welfare Canada, Ottawa.

Lindsay, Anne. *The Lighthearted Cookbook: Recipes for Healthy Heart Cooking.* Key Porter Books, 1988.

Oliver, Margo. *Margo Oliver's Cookbook For Seniors: Nutritious Recipes for One, Two, or More.* Self-Counsel Press, 1989.

FINDING SERVICES

Mr. Nobody. National Film Board video No. X 0187 100.

Seniors' Guide to Federal Programs and Services. Handbook. Health and Welfare Canada, 1988.

SENIORS' SELF-HELP

Discover Choices: A Program for People 55 Years and Over. A kit comprising 23 articles on many aspects of aging, almost all written by elders. Health and Welfare Canada, 1988.

Senior Connection, The. Manual for personal growth and senior peer helping. Senior Peer Helping Centre, Etobicoke, Ont.

Appendix C

Other Resources

Elders are often revitalized by realizing they can still learn new skills and play a role in ordering society in general and their own future in particular. There are many organizations they can join to help themselves do this.

The best place to start a search for an appropriate group may well be the New Horizons Program run by Health and Welfare Canada, which funds all kinds of activities and facilities for seniors. Contact the national office at 6th Floor, Brooke Claxton Building, Tunney's Pasture, Ottawa, K1A 1B5, or regional offices in Vancouver, Edmonton, Regina, Winnipeg, Toronto, Montreal, Moncton, Halifax, Charlottetown, or St. John's.

One of the most extensive and best known educational organizations for those 60 and older is Elderhostel, which sponsors inexpensive, short-term academic programs, both in Canada and in many other countries. For more information, ask for its catalogue at your library or write to Elderhostel Canada, Suite 300, 33 Prince Arthur Avenue, Toronto, Ontario, M5R 1B2. There are also regional Elderhostel offices in Fort Smith, N.W.T., Penticton, B.C., Calgary, Sudbury, Montreal, and Halifax.

Of the numerous associations that exist for elders interested in political action, one of the largest and best known is the Canadian Association of Retired Persons. At time of writing, CARP has some 40,000 members making their views known on many matters concerning older people. Write to the head office at 27 Queen Street East, Suite 304, Toronto, Ontario, M5C 2M6, or contact any one of the local chapters in Armdale, N.S., Nepean, Thornhill, Burlington, Hamilton, and St. Catharines in Ontario, and Saskatoon, Regina, and Vancouver.

Among organizations running recreational and social programs, two of the larger and more active are the Golden Age Association in Montreal, which has a main centre, four minicentres, and 10 clubs in many parts of the city, and the Second Mile Club of Toronto, which has seven centres around the city.

The Canadian Institute of Senior Centres can direct you to clubs right across the country. Write the CISC at 500 Danforth Avenue, Suite 112, Toronto, Ontario, M4K 1P6. And at least one province, Ontario, has an association of clubs. If you live in that province, contact the Older Adult Centres Association of Ontario at 1220 Sheppard Avenue East, Willowdale, Ontario, M2K 2X1.